Series / Number 02-039

The Study of Soviet Foreign Policy:
Decision-Theory-Related Approaches

ARNOLD L. HORELICK,
A. ROSS JOHNSON and
JOHN D. STEINBRUNER
The Rand Corporation

 SAGE PUBLICATIONS / Beverly Hills / London

For information address:

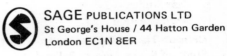

SAGE PUBLICATIONS, INC.
275 South Beverly Drive
Beverly Hills, California 90212

SAGE PUBLICATIONS LTD
St George's House / 44 Hatton Garden
London EC1N 8ER

International Standard Book Number 0-8039-0595-5

Library of Congress Catalog Card No. 75-34540

FIRST PRINTING

When citing a professional paper, please use the proper form. Remember to cite the correct Sage Professional Paper series title and include the paper number. One of the two following formats can be adapted (depending on the style manual used):

(1) AZAR, E. E. (1972) "International Events Interaction Analysis." Sage Professional Papers in International Studies, 1, 02-001. Beverly Hills and London: Sage Pubns.

OR

(2) Azar, Edward E. 1972. *International Events Interaction Analysis*. Sage Professional Papers in International Studies, vol. 1, series no. 02-001. Beverly Hills and London: Sage Publications.

CONTENTS

AUTHORS' NOTES: *This report reviews recent scholarly literature on decision-making and Soviet foreign policy, with particular reference to Soviet crisis behavior. The review was undertaken to assess the utility of this literature for policy analysts concerned with Soviet affairs.*

Section II was contributed by John D. Steinbruner, Associate Professor of Public Policy at Harvard University and Consultant to The Rand Corporation. Arnold L. Horelick and A. Ross Johnson, members of Rand's Social Science Department, collaborated on Secs. III and IV.

The authors are indebted to the following individuals for detailed criticisms of earlier drafts of this report: Hannes Jurgen Adomeit, University of Glasgow; Garry D. Brewer, The Rand Corporation; William A. Welsh, University of Iowa; and to other readers including William Jones, Ralph Strauch, and Thomas W. Wolfe of The Rand Corporation. Our study benefited from a bibliographic review of recent Soviet foreign policy studies undertaken by Jan F. Triska of Stanford University. Lilita Dzirkals, The Rand Corporation, provided extensive bibliographic and other research assistance.

These acknowledgments are not intended to associate any of the readers either with treatment of individual works or with the general conclusions and recommendations in this report; for these the co-authors alone are responsible.

ARNOLD L. HORELICK is a Senior Social Scientist and member of the Social Science Department at The Rand Corporation and has been visiting professor of political science at UCLA, Columbia, Hunter College (CUNY), and California Institute of Technology. He is coauthor (with Myron Rush) of Strategic Power and Soviet Foreign Policy, *University of Chicago Press (1966) and other monographs on Soviet foreign and military policy.*

A. ROSS JOHNSON is a Senior Social Scientist and Associate Head, Social Science Department, at The Rand Corporation. He is the author of The Transformation of Ideology: The Yugoslav Case, *M.I.T. Press (1972),* Yugoslavia: In the Twilight of Tito, *Sage Publications (1974) and other monographs on East European political and military affairs. He received his Ph.D. from Columbia University.*

JOHN D. STEINBRUNER is Associate Professor of Public Policy at the John F. Kennedy School of Government, and Assistant Director of the Program for Science and International Affairs both at Harvard University. Author of The Cybernetic Theory of Decision: New Dimensions of Political Analysis, *Princeton University Press (1974), he received his Ph.D. from M.I.T.*

I. INTRODUCTION

Studies of the external behavior of foreign states undertaken by political analysts have been faulted by a number of academic critics for disregarding promising new developments in social science theory and methodology.[1] The research reported here addresses one specific question posed by critics: are there models of decisionmaking in the social sciences which could help practicing analysts to improve their understanding and anticipation of Soviet foreign policy behavior, particularly in crises?

In Sec. II we review the theoretical literature on decisionmaking in the social sciences. We ask how it can contribute to the work of the foreign policy analyst. The decisionmaking literature is vast, and its boundaries within the social sciences are disputed. Since a comprehensive review of this literature would be incompatible with the purpose of and the resources available to this research, we have undertaken a selective and interpretive examination. We offer a categorization of selected decisionmaking studies that we believe to be both original and appropriate to our research purpose.

In Sec. III, we review the Western literature on Soviet foreign policy decisionmaking in terms of its utility to the foreign affairs analyst. Sovietology itself has been widely criticized in recent years for remaining outside the mainstream of modern social science. Indeed, as viewed by their critics, academic Sovietologists have stood closer in their approach to journalists and government analysts than to social scientists. Only in the last decade have some Sovietologists (and their colleagues analyzing other Communist countries) concerned themselves with bridging that gap.

"Decisionmaking" is not necessarily the most useful prism through which to critique Sovietology; it was imposed by the central research question. The body of literature reviewed in Sec. III is far smaller, less well developed, and more tentative than that examined in Sec. II. In order to illustrate the few attempts to apply a decisionmaking approach and some of the other innovative currents of Sovietology that have appeared since the mid-1960s, we necessarily discuss individual works in greater detail. Some of these—by virtue of poor research design, lack of internal consistency, and absence of observable linkage between underlying assumptions, empirical data marshalled, and articulated hypotheses—do not meet high scholarly standards. Although we are more interested in highlighting promising approaches than in criticizing their performance records to date, we point out serious failings in the latter where they clearly exist.

We stress the special purpose of this review. The foreign policy analyst is not concerned with the theory building enterprise *per se* or with the expansion of knowledge "for its own sake." His task is to improve the understanding of, and, if possible, to anticipate particular foreign policy behaviors of other states in specific circumstances and under specified conditions.

The foreign policy analyst seeks to understand the interrelationships among a large number of influences shaping specific foreign policies of a state. The unfolding of a particular policy will always be contingent on a larger historical and international context which usually precludes prediction of specific outcomes with high confidence. The analyst is properly concerned with anticipating the salient alterna-

---

[1] See, for example, Pool (1972), p. 292.

tive directions in which a particular foreign policy may develop and, drawing on his specialized knowledge and some assumptions about context (e.g., policies of other states, including his own), with attempting to rank these possibilities according to order of probability. The analyst with greater understanding and knowledge will presumably make such contingent predictions more successfully over time.

The working style of the foreign policy analyst is inherently integrative, combining specific information (often of uncertain validity) with more general knowledge about a specific country and some fundamental premises about international affairs in order to estimate the import and interrelationship of complex events and processes. Familiarity with social science theory may enhance and inform this integrative function.

Social science theory offers no panacea to the foreign policy analyst. There are no developed models of foreign policy decisionmaking. Nor do refined and validated theoretical building blocks await a clever model-maker. Developed models of foreign policy decisionmaking could in any case serve the foreign affairs analyst only by providing a useful perspective; it must be remembered that, by definition, models are imperfect representations of selected aspects of reality. The foreign policy analyst must be concerned with the total behavior of a foreign state, not some arbitrary aspects of it.

If the social sciences cannot revolutionize the work of the foreign policy analyst, they may sharpen his existing tools and suggest new ones. More explicit concern with the logic of inquiry and formal analytical techniques may help the analyst to broaden his intellectual horizons, sensitize him to new alternative explanations or lead him to discard sterile ones, impel him to formulate more salient questions, suggest the relevance of and help him to organize new classes of data, allow him to extrapolate more meaningfully on the basis of partial data, and generally provide him with better criteria for distinguishing "signals" from "noise" in the flood of information that crosses his desk. New social science theory can help him to reexamine the appropriateness of habitual patterns of analysis. All these insights can broaden and deepen the foreign policy analyst's capacity for creative judgment—which will remain the central element of his art.[2]

In this spirit we review the decisionmaking literature and its as yet limited applications in Soviet studies. We reject both the hucksterism of some social scientists and the inflexible defense of the status quo by some practitioners that have burdened discussions of the application of social science methodology to the daily business of foreign policy analysts. We do not ask the impossible of the literature reviewed here: that it should provide a key to comprehensive and consistent explanations or accurate and reliable predictions of the conduct of Soviet foreign policy. From our own collective perspective, which includes familiarity with policy analysis in general and experience analyzing Soviet and East European foreign policies in particular, we assess the utility of the literature for the analyst of Soviet foreign policy. We believe that the present level of performance by the foreign affairs analyst can be raised. We believe that more attention to the literature on decisionmaking (or what we term here "decision-theory-related literature") may help. But we do not assume a *priori* that an alternative approach is an improvement over those utilized to date merely because it is different.

Our conclusions about the utility of the general literature on decisionmaking for applied purposes of foreign policy analysis and suggestions for improvement are formulated at the end of Sec. II. Specific conclusions about its applications to Sovietology will be found at the end of Sec. III. Section IV is devoted to recommended

---

[2] Some of these issues are discussed further in Millikan (1959) and in Strauch (1973).

directions of future work which could enhance the utility of this literature for the applied purposes of foreign policy analysis.

A few definitions are in order at the outset of this review. Our use of the term "decisionmaking," and what is central and peripheral to the concept, is explained on pp. 4-5.[3] Following Kaplan (1964), we distinguish between "methods" (approaches) and "techniques" (the tools for applying those methods). We draw on Kuhn (1963) in distinguishing among "methods" (which we generally label "approaches") as between models, theories, and paradigms.

[3] An introduction to the decisionmaking approach can be found in Rosenau (1969), pp. 167-174.

II. MODELS OF DECISION IN THE SOCIAL SCIENCES

INTRODUCTION

What help does the literature on decisionmaking offer to an analyst who wishes to understand the external behavior of foreign governments, particularly the Soviet Union, and especially in times of crisis? The question itself presents major problems.

Under any broad definition of the topic, the literature on decisionmaking is truly vast—involving a number of well developed areas of several disciplines. To probe deeply into all its dimensions would be a prodigious undertaking out of proportion to the objectives and resources of this study. A number of reviews are available[4] which summarize parts of the literature and provide extensive references. None of these is completely comprehensive, and naturally enough none focuses directly on the problem of utilizing the literature for the practical purpose suggested.

Take, for example, the question of crisis behavior. There is some attempt in the literature to determine the properties of crises and to analyze the peculiarities of decisions taken in crises. These studies will be mentioned briefly. A number of "case" studies of actual crises are also examined. The main theoretical literature, however, does not invest the distinction between crisis and non-crisis with fundamental significance. Decision processes go to the very core of human capacities. The mechanisms of decision in humans and in their institutions do not change their basic character under crisis, even though the behavior they generate may change very sharply. Most of the literature focuses on fundamental assumptions involved in the theory of decision without introducing the special case of crisis For the policy analyst concerned above all with specific outcomes of the decision process under circumstances in which the behavior of decisionmakers is subjected to the special stress of crisis, the failure of the main theoretical literature to explore the effects of crisis conditions diminishes its utility.

The review undertaken here attempts to be reasonably broad but not exhaustive. It focuses on major works of particular utility and does not presume to cover the full literature underpinning the various topics raised. Inevitably, such a selective enterprise entails the exercise of a great deal of individual judgment and interpretation. To help the reader follow our selective judgments, some of the unresolved problems in the decisionmaking literature are outlined below.

Theories of decision constitute only one approach to foreign or domestic policy analysis, and it is important to distinguish decisionmaking from the large class of phenomena whereby the behavior of governments and the events of history are determined. For the typical policy problem we can distinguish among (a) actors, (b) values (or objectives), (c) information, (d) options, (e) the state-of-the-world (environment), (f) the decision process, (g) the decision, (h) the process of implementation, and (i) the actual outcome. Models of decision concern processes which occur at (f) and (h). Such processes integrate elements falling under categories (a), (b), (c), and (d) to produce decisions and become an element in the longer flow of causal forces in the environment (e) which produce outcomes (i). There are important distinctions belonging to categories (a) through (e) which do not directly impinge upon the topic of decisionmaking, though no realistic analysis of an actual decision could possibly proceed without taking them into consideration.

---

[4] Becker and McClintock (1967), Edwards (1961), May (1974), Rapoport and Wallsten (1972), Shubik and Brewer (1972 a and b).

The driving purpose is also an important determinant of decisionmaking analyses. Theoretical approaches to decisionmaking are generally distinguishable in terms of the nature of the basic argument. Some theories are advanced as normative statements of how decisions ought to be made with no necessary implication that they actually are made in that way. Other theories are descriptive—that is, they make empirical claims setting forth a theoretical account of how decisions actually are made under rules of evidence which allow for the possibility that theoretical assumptions may be disconfirmed by actual observations. Still other theories are tautological in nature in that they posit ideal assumptions which are used to interpret evidence. Under this latter procedure, the central propositions of the theory are assumed to be true by definition, and the purpose of analysis is to build a coherent picture of an actual decision in terms of the theoretical assumptions. In tautological usage, in other words, the assumptions themselves are not called into question.

These purposive distinctions do not drastically affect the basic logic of a theory of decision, for the same theoretical assumptions may be treated in all three approaches. Indeed, the distinctions themselves are not absolute. A normative model which had no empirical validity whatsoever would be quickly rejected as irrelevant and useless. Similarly, a model with empirical validity is very likely to embody some normative claim. Thanks presumably to the process of natural selection, we do not find many human beings using a decision process which is wildly unsuccessful. Nevertheless, the distinctions among the driving purposes underlying various analyses significantly affect the relationship between theory and evidence and thus the practical application of a given theory.

If the analyst is particularly concerned with predicting the flow of events (including probable consequences of various policy options), then the tautological form of analysis is clearly the most useful. The problem for the analyst is largely a matter of anticipating the decisions of pertinent actors other than his client, the decisionmaker. Normative analysis is essentially designed to impose consistency and efficiency on the client; it leaves open the question as to how other actors will behave. A descriptive model with established validity would be ideal, of course, but such a model is not to be found at the current state of the art. Available descriptive models tend to be narrow in scope, demanding in terms of the amount and type of data required for their application, and weak in the predictive power they confer. Given these difficulties, the tautological use of decision theory for prediction becomes virtually inevitable. Some framework of interpretation is needed to give coherence to inherently ambiguous events and to provide more penetrating predictions than a blind projection of past trends. Whether acknowledged or not, a theory of the decision process used tautologically generally underlies policy analysis.

The obvious problem with the tautological procedure is that a plausible, theoretically coherent analysis might turn out to be badly misleading in real-world terms, as does indeed happen with discouraging regularity. To mitigate this effect, the review emphasizes competitive theoretical accounts of the decision process (which tend to yield conflicting explanations and predictions when used as the basis for policy analysis) and suggests the importance of competitive analysis.

Related to distinctions of logical purpose are differing levels of articulation at which theories of the decision process are worked out. The literature makes important distinctions between paradigms, theories, and models. Of these, the most specific and completely articulated is a model. A *model* can be defined as a system of logical relationships—expressed in terms of equations, explicit assertions, or even physical components—which is coherent, consistent, and internally complete.[5] Per-

---

[5] Nagel (1961).

haps the clearest example of a model is provided by a computer program simulating some decision processes.[6] A *theory* is more general and less completely defined. It involves a set of assumptions and general inferences which have basic coherence and consistency, but which usually defy complete enumeration or specificity. Deterrence theory is a prominent example: it is easy to state its central propositions but very difficult to capture all of its assumptions and implicit inferences. The word *paradigm* refers to a yet more fundamental level of critical assumptions which provides the base for building theories.[7] A paradigm can generate a number of theories. Theories, which have some focused application, are in essence an elaboration of paradigm assumptions. A theory based on a particular paradigm can give rise to a number of different models.

The natural sciences have developed theories of high quality. In, say, physics, one encounters theories of great precision and general applicability which yield accurate predictions. The social sciences have not developed theories of comparable quality. There are theories, of course, but they are much more restricted in their application, much less precise in their analysis, much less powerful as devices for prediction. To a large extent, work in the social sciences proceeds by building theories which are reasonably specific to the task at hand. Thus Newhouse's (1973) analysis of the U.S. decision process leading to the SALT I agreement includes a number of statements which are theoretical in kind and which share important assumptions with other analyses of different decisions. Newhouse's analysis is specific enough to the topic; however, his theoretical statements cannot be easily and directly applied to other events.

Given this situation, significant discourse in the social sciences concerning decisionmaking tends to occur at the paradigm level of articulation. That, at any rate, is the basic assumption of this review. This assumption generates three central propositions: (1) that virtually all policy analysis depends upon an identifiable base paradigm; (2) that the most fundamental categorization of the decisionmaking literature is in terms of base paradigms; (3) that an important development in the literature over recent decades has been the gradual emergence of an alternative base paradigm to the dominant conception of rational choice.

BASE PARADIGMS

Two fundamental paradigms can be identified in the decisionmaking literature.[8] The first of these is embodied in what is generally known as the rational theory of decision. In order to denote the underlying paradigm and to avoid some of the difficulties of the word "rational," that paradigm is labeled the "analytic paradigm." It clearly occupies the dominant position in the literature and provides the basis for most policy analysis.

The second basic paradigm can be labeled the "cybernetic paradigm." It diverges from the basic assumptions of the analytic paradigm, and it generates theories of simple decision mechanisms which are nonetheless highly adaptive under proper conditions. It is far less developed as a base for policy analysis, but it is promising because of the problems which have been encountered in analytic theories.

6. Crecine (1969), Cyert and March (1963).
7. Kuhn (1963).
8. See Steinbruner (1974).

The Analytic Paradigm

The basic conception of rational choice involves a decisionmaker acting to maximize his values given the constraints which he faces. Models and theories of decision belonging to the rational tradition seek to give a coherent account of this process. The problem with the word "rational," however, is that it cannot be separated in Western culture from an evaluation of outcome. "Rational" clearly suggests that whatever policy promises to produce the "best" results is most worthy of approval. Decision processes which seek to approximate the assumptions of rational choice models may or may not produce the "best" results.[9] To avoid inevitable confusion, the word "analytic" is adopted to label this genre of theory. The label reflects the basic character of the decision process pictured by this kind of theory—that is, an explicit breaking down of the decision problems into its components and a deliberate process of aggregation to achieve a decision.

The theories and models of decision which belong to this category all share a set of underlying assumptions which serve to define the paradigm:

1. The decisionmaker somehow integrates incommensurate dimensions of value in order to produce a preference ordering for alternative states of the world.

2. The decisionmaker makes direct calculations of the possible outcome of alternative actions and somehow makes probabilistic judgments about the likelihood of each occurring.

3. The decisionmaker somehow integrates his preferences and outcome judgments to produce a decision which is optimal by the calculation he uses.

In cases where the decision process consists of a series of related decisions extending over time, there is an additional assumption; namely:

4. The decisionmaker somehow updates his calculations as new information becomes available.

These assumptions[10] all pertain to individual decisionmakers for the obvious reason that only individuals display the degree of integration and behavioral coherence necessary to sustain such a process. The basic conception of decisionmaking—and in some sense its ultimate locus in the real world—is to be found at the level of single individuals. That fact in turn poses difficulties for analytic decision theories applied to collective decision processes.

Analytic Theories of Individual Decision

The clearest and most rigorous embodiments of the analytic paradigm are to be found in formal axiom systems which describe the decision process with respect to highly stylized hypothetical problems.[11] These systems are closely related to the fundamental logic of measurement,[12] which is itself one of the central components of all scientific thought. This highly abstract and esoteric dimension of the literature is far removed from the concrete problems which beset the foreign policy analyst. Axiomatic systems do provide the analytic paradigms and the topic of decisionmaking as a whole with a clear, rigorous, core logic, and an intellectually compelling

[9] In quantitative presentations of the theory, an optimum point is often identified which does define the best result within a restricted set of assumptions. For actual decisions, however, it can never be demonstrated that all pertinent aspects of the problem are captured within any given measurement scheme, and it is always an open question whether an outcome which appears optimal within a given set of calculations is actually optimal in a global sense.

[10] For more detailed treatment, see Steinbruner (1974).

[11] Luce and Raiffa (1957), Luce and Suppes (1965), Savage (1959), von Neumann and Morgenstern (1954), and Wald (1950).

[12] Krantz, Luce, Suppes and Tversky (1971).

structure to impose on the fluid, intellectually recalcitrant problems of the empirical order.

Extensive attempts have been made to work out descriptive or empirical models consistent with the axiom systems and to test these against actual decisionmaking behavior, usually in a highly controlled laboratory setting. Extensive reviews of this literature including bibliographies are available,[13] and these efforts need not be duplicated here. This literature yields a few generalizations, which must be advanced with great caution:

1. In all but the very simplest and most highly structured of decision problems, actual behavior violates the major axioms used in formal models (e.g., assumptions of transitivity and the independence of numerical measures for utility and probability), and deviates sharply from the predictions of at least the simplest and most straightforward of these models.[14]

2. A number of stochastic models using rather advanced statistical techniques have been advanced in an attempt to gain greater explanatory and predictive power,[15] but as yet without striking success.

3. Despite this general trend in the literature, some impressive results with expected value models (the simplest of the formal models) have been obtained in psychological experiments involving signal detection problems (which are binary choice decisions).[16] Normal decisionmakers can be taught to use a decision process approximating the formal models and under some circumstances they do so naturally. The weight of experimental evidence indicates, however, that at least at their present state of development, formal models of decision of the analytic variety do not capture some of the most consequential processes of decision which operate in the empirical world.

There have been a number of successful and influential theoretical developments which have been principally inspired by the formal analytic models of decision. The most famous of these is undoubtedly microeconomics, where the entire framework of analysis depends critically upon assumptions that both the consumers and the supplier firms of a competitive market behave in accord with analytic assumptions.[17] This is far too large a field to be incorporated in this review. It should be noted, however, that the academic success of microeconomics—a required course in virtually all graduate and undergraduate programs in economics—lends substantial momentum to the analytic paradigm as the established position in the theory of decision.

A related development has created what may be termed the art of policy analysis. Using the normative form of argument, microeconomic analysis has been extended to the public sector and applied to policy problems which are not completely governed by a market mechanism. This has produced systems analysis as an established professional subfield;[18] it has also inspired theoretical discussions of the public sector budget process[19] and the budget reform movement, "Program, Planning, Budgeting."[20] These developments arose from arguments that the governmental process ought to be analytic in character, but tends not to be under normal conditions.

[13] Becker and McClintock (1967), Edwards (1961), and Rapoport and Wallsten (1972).

[14] Becker and McClintock (1967), Rapoport and Wallsten (1972), and Simon (1959).

[15] Reviewed in Becker and McClintock (1967), and Rapoport and Wallsten (1972).

[16] Becker and McClintock (1967), and Swets, Tanner, and Birdsall (1968).

[17] Braff (1969), Dorfman (1964), Koopmans (1957), and Samuelson (1970).

[18] Hitch and McKean (1965), McKean (1958), Novick (1965), and Quade (1964).

[19] Novick (1965), and Schultze (1968).

[20] Haveman and Margolis (1970), Lyden and Miller (1968), Novick (1965), and Schultze (1968).

Development of basic analytic decision models has also produced mathematical programming and the various quantitative techniques known as operations research,[21] which have found extensive application to a variety of practical decision problems. Again, the basic argument is normative in character. The quantitative procedures have been applied with some success to actual decision problems, though these are usually well structured, highly constrained problems of lesser significance in terms of policy.[22]

Applying mathematical analysis to the problem of decision, theorists in the analytic tradition have built a compelling theoretical structure. They have not been successful, however, in establishing direct empirical relationships and cannot provide the explanatory and predictive power which mathematics has given in physics, for example. Analytic decision theories do not constitute a science, even though they have some attributes of theoretical rigor.

This situation makes tautological application of analytic decision theories both inevitable and desirable. The highly developed theoretical structure which is offered is unquestionably useful in organizing and enlightening the judgmental process of arriving at explanations and predictions of complex events. Again, the analyst needs *some* framework of assumptions for his work. And, since the analytic paradigm provides what is by far the most developed framework, it is naturally used.

The prime example of analytic decision theory developed through a tautological argument is undoubtedly the theory of deterrence.[23] As a practical variant of the formal theory of games (part of the axiomatic development of the paradigm),[24] deterrence theory assumes that the adversary is aptly characterized as an analytic decisionmaker and conducts its analysis by developing the logic, the policy, and the concrete actions required to deter such a decisionmaker. The arguments thus derived have had considerable influence and have proven useful in structuring problems of force posture and weapons procurement.[25] The empirical validity of the logic is assumed rather than demonstrated, but in the absence of competing assumptions, and as long as general war is avoided, that leap of faith is widely accepted.

Theories of bargaining and strategic interactions are another example. Using the logic of analytic decision theory, Schelling (1960) and others have worked out an analysis of adversary relationships which provides a coherent account of the tactics, maneuverings, and bargaining behavior in which persons in conflict can be expected to engage.[26] Highly plausible real-world examples are legion. In providing a coherent picture of the bargaining process, these theories are helpful in guiding an analyst in making predictions even though, again, they have not generated empirically validated calculations.

As noted, the obvious problem with tautologous use of analytic logic is that, although it may be plausible and coherent, it also could turn out to be badly misleading, since the question of empirical validity remains so open. Allison (1971) has waged an attack on these grounds. He has pointed out that much analysis of the behavior of governments has rested upon the assumption that they act as if they were a unitary rational actor, as a single individual making deliberate calculations in pursuit of clear objectives. Such analysis can be seen as a loose derivation from the core logic of analytic decision theory. It is obviously a gross simplification, since

[21] Baumol (1972), Dorfman, Samuelson, and Solow, (1958), and Morse and Kimball (1951).

[22] Morse and Kimball (1951).

[23] Kahn (1961), and Snyder (1961).

[24] Luce and Raiffa (1957), and von Neumann and Morgenstern (1954).

[25] Enthoven and Smith (1971), and U.S. Congress (1968).

[26] See also Iklé (1964), and Schultze (1968).

no government displays such coherence. Allison, stating a major counter-theme in the literature (discussed below), argues strongly for disaggregating such an obvious collective as an entire government into components which might more believably approximate the coherence of a single actor. This step, which does hedge against gross misestimation, renders any analysis far more complicated and predictions far more difficult.

Analytic Theories of Collective Decision

Formidable logical barriers are encountered in attempting to extend the analytic models of decision to the collective level of explanation. The articulation of axiomatic theories is such that interpersonal comparisons of utility values cannot be made, that is, one person's unit of value does not necessarily equal another's, and hence they cannot be validly added.[27] Arrow (1961) has demonstrated that, given this fact and given a reasonable set of restrictions, there is no voting arrangement which will give a reliable procedure for generating collective decisions. This result blocks one of the most obvious and appealing approaches to the problem.[28] Moreover, problems of market externalities and public goods[29] prevent application of standard market analysis to many issues of public policy. The Pareto criterion for social choice, which has received wide attention from economists because it avoids interpersonal utility comparisons,[30] is too restrictive to apply to many (if any) major policy issues.[31] It is plagued by the "second-best theorem" which, in restricting formal analysis to the situation where the conditions of optimality are all achieved simultaneously, sows confusion as to how to proceed in the practical world when such a procedure is obviously impractical.[32] The concept "willingness to pay"[33] helps overcome the problem of interpersonal utility comparisons, but since it entails a non-coercive tax system, it provides an unfortunate incentive for everyone to conceal what he is willing to pay. Rothenberg (1961) cuts through these difficulties by evoking the long-discussed proposition that society as a whole has social preferences which do not depend upon aggregating individual preferences, but this resolution seems to put the analysis back into the theoretical framework discussed under individual decision models.

Thus, treatment of collective decision problems in the analytic tradition proceeds on the basis of individual decision models—by means of market analysis where that can be justified, by treating the collective as an individual entity, by theories of bargaining among individuals, and by descriptive models of voting. The first three procedures are discussed above. Voting (although more removed from issues of foreign policy decisionmaking) also deserves brief mention.

A number of descriptive (empirical) approaches to the phenomena of voting have been inspired by analytic models of decision applied to voters, candidates, and elected officials. Downs (1957) provides such a theory which is empirical in spirit, though he does not in fact collect the pertinent data. Riker (1961, 1962) provides a review and a theory of the formation of political coalitions by analytic voters.

[27] Edwards (1954), and Luce and Raiffa (1957).

[28] Even if cardinal utility measures (i.e., ones with equal units) are assumed to exist, Arrow's result will still obtain if individual preferences do not meet some reasonably restrictive constraints.

[29] Baumol (1952), and Olson (1965).

[30] The Pareto criterion holds that a decision ought to be taken if it leaves all the members of a population at least as well off as they were prior to the decision and improves the lot of some. See Baumol (1952) and Buchanan and Tullach (1967).

[31] Steiner (1970).

[32] Baumol (1952).

[33] Samuelson (1954).

In general, if the collective decision problem is understood as that of giving an account of how individual decisionmakers act collectively (as opposed to treating the collective as an entity which acts like an individual), then the analytic paradigm encounters serious logical difficulties.

These difficulties, it seems fair to say, have prevented analytic theories of collective choice from playing the powerful organizing role that analytic theories of individual decision have played. The formal logic of decision provides a clear conceptual base for the policy analyst from which to approach the inherently confusing complexities of the empirical world, and hence the presence of anomalies and confusion in the core logic would seem to be seriously debilitating. The proposition cannot be proved, of course, since so much depends upon the judgments analysts make in applying the logical structure to concrete problems, and the process of judgment has not been recorded (and perhaps cannot be). Still, at the current state of the art, it seems clear that the main thrust of the analytic paradigm is developed from its conceptions of individual choice.

The Cybernetic Paradigm

The problem with the analytic paradigm, as widely pointed out,[34] is that its assumptions seem to require very extensive calculations on the part of the decisionmaker, calculations which can readily be shown to be impossibly burdensome. Since human beings (and, indeed, other organisms) are nonetheless able to make decisions easily and successfully in most circumstances, this argument leads to the strong suspicion that at least many decision processes must work in a much less burdensome way.

This argument has led many expositors of analytic logic to introduce limitations on the analytic process in order to achieve decision models which sharply reduce the assumed burdens of processing information. Simon's (1957) famous satisficing model and his more general conception of bounded rationality represent perhaps the clearest articulation of this theme. It is possible, however, to conceive of a more radical shift in analytic assumptions than these efforts entail and to project a completely separate paradigm of the decision process. This tendency is palpable in the literature at the moment. Steinbruner (1974) labels the alternative position the "cybernetic paradigm" to reflect the core logic of this position. Cybernetics, as herein conceived, offers theories of very simple decision mechanisms which are nonetheless highly successful in the proper environments.

Since the cybernetic paradigm is in some dimensions less developed and is at any rate less recognized than the analytic paradigm, the definition of what it includes is inherently more controversial. Nonetheless, a set of critical assumptions can be identified which reveal the spirit of this approach:
1.   The decisionmaker strains to avoid direct outcome calculations and thus to eliminate the impact of uncertainty.
2.   The essence of the decision process is the performance of a set of procedures (as opposed to the pursuit of preferred outcomes).
3.   The decisionmaker is sensitive to a very limited range of information defined in terms of pertinence to the established procedures.

The procedures performed by such a decisionmaker do in fact produce outcomes, though these are not *intended* in any strict sense of the word. In cases where the decisionmaker operates successfully, the environment is usually structured such

---

[34] Lindblom (1959, 1965), and Simon (1968).

that there is a feedback loop connecting the effects produced by the decision process and the information input of subsequent stages.

Clearly a decision process operating in accord with these assumptions would not need to integrate incommensurate values, would not require a preference ordering, and would not involve probabilistic judgments of various outcome possibilities. In other words, the cybernetic paradigm specifically challenges the central assumptions of the analytic paradigm.

The most familiar and most rigorously developed presentations of cybernetic assumptions occur in contexts where decision mechanisms are embedded in larger systems whose design is known. This is the format, for example, in which mathematical control theory has been developed.[35] In that context cybernetic assumptions at least approach the rigor of formal analytic models, but they have not drawn a great deal of attention from decision theorists, probably because this analysis from a systems viewpoint appears rather deterministic—not the business of those who concern themselves with theories of choice. Deutsch's famous work (1963) applies cybernetic ideas from this literature to political analysis. His work takes a general systems point of view and does not develop an analysis of the major issues of decision theory.

If the larger system is essentially unknown and if the comprehensive knowledge is not available which makes decisionmaking behavior within the system appear deterministic, then cybernetic analysis rather clearly belongs to decision theory. It generates theories of choice which are quite distinct from those of the analytic paradigm. Ashby (1952, 1970) and Beer (1959) are perhaps the clearest proponents of this latter perspective. Simon (1968) contributes an important analysis of the environmental structure upon which cybernetic analysis seems to depend. Alexander (1968) analyzes the workings of cybernetic processes in architectural design. Steinbruner (1974) develops the logic of the paradigm in relation to analytic assumptions.

One can find descriptive models of individual choice belonging to the cybernetic paradigm in learning theory in psychology.[36] The principles of conditioning, which have been the subject of extensive empirical work, can be associated with the cybernetic paradigm, and accounts of higher order behavior based on these principles would presumably provide the basis for empirical analysis based on cybernetic assumptions.[37] Extensive review would, however, be required to sort out the work in the learning theory literature which is pertinent to the theory of decision. At any rate, the state of development of empirical models is certainly no greater than that of the empirical models belonging to the analytic tradition.

Since the spirit of the cybernetic paradigm is to fragment a decision problem into small manageable pieces (which are then treated separately and not integrated as in the analytic tradition), it seems to yield a less troubled conception of collective decisionmaking. Separate decisionmakers control separate dimensions of the problem; in the absence of any requirements for integration, comparisons between them are unnecessary. The collective decision process becomes just that—collective but not aggregated.

Cyert and March (1963) have provided an account of organizational procedures which roughly fits within the cybernetic paradigm. Their core model of individual choice is akin to Simon's satisficing model. On that basis they describe a sequential process whereby decisions are broken down into components corresponding to or-

[35] Bellman (1961), Riggs (1970), and Weiner (1961).
[36] Kimble (1961).
[37] Skinner (1957).

ganizational sub-units; the separate components are decided as they arise, with no overall integration. A number of studies have simulated budget processes with models of this sort,[38] and these show that for short periods of time one can track the flow of actual budget decisions.

Lindblom (1959, 1965) has made a related argument in a broader political context. He suggests that most decisions proceed via small, marginal changes in established policies or actions as a means of coping with the problems of uncertainty and value conflict. Decisions are reached in ignorance of their direct effects and of the reactions of other decisionmakers whose interests are involved. If the effects turn out to be acceptable, the course is pursued with further marginal decisions; if not, then something new is tried. This, he argues, is the way a political collective gropes its way forward; a process which he labels partisan mutual adjustment. In the general literature this process has become known as "incrementalism," reflecting the slow evolutionary changes in outcome which are often seen as the signature of this kind of decisionmaking.

The core logic of these approaches derives from the cybernetic paradigm, although that derivation is not well articulated by either Cyert and March or Lindblom. Both of these central sources have essentially constructed their analyses as arguments against dominant analytic assumptions. The chief effect of this is that the significance of incrementally evolving outcomes is overemphasized. An outcome stream changing over time in small marginal increments can result from either an analytic or a cybernetic decision process, and it is not the only pattern which the cybernetic process produces.[39]

The organizational analysis suggested by Cyert and March has been developed by Allison (1971) as an approach to governmental decisionmaking, including crisis issues. Allison demonstrates that sharp differences in analysis result when this approach is adopted as a framework for analysis, rather than some variant of the analytic paradigm. This perspective, which he labels Model II, emphasizes the effects of routine procedures in organizations and seems to explain thereby many events which are highly anomalous when viewed from an analytic perspective. Marshall (1966, 1971) had earlier argued the importance of this organizational process approach in understanding foreign governments and in assessing Soviet military power in particular.

It must be recognized that the cybernetic paradigm has not fully developed the carefully articulated theoretical coherence which has made the analytic paradigm a powerful tool for intellectual organization. Nor has it as yet spawned much applied analysis of significant issues. Promising development has occurred at both levels, however, and a fully coherent competitor to the established analytic paradigm seems to be emerging.

The Benefits of Competition

The distinction between the analytic and the cybernetic paradigm is presented here more sharply than it usually appears in the general literature. Writers in the analytic tradition generally strain to incorporate the arguments of cybernetic analysis without abandoning analytic assumptions—by introducing various constraints and qualifications to those assumptions. This reflects a laudable instinct for theoretical order, but under such a procedure the analyst loses the potential benefits of competition.

---

[38] Crecine (1969), and Davis, Dempster, and Wildavsky (1966).

[39] See Steinbruner (1974).

It cannot be denied that the core logic of the two paradigms differs very sharply. Except for the simplest and most highly structured problems, they help generate very different interpretations of the same events, very different predictions of future events. President Kennedy's actions at the Nassau Conference in 1962, for example, are frequently cited as a case of puzzling foreign policy behavior. To those using analytic assumptions as the basis for analysis, the President appeared to be tearing up elaborately constructed policies for reasons difficult to fathom. When approached from a cybernetic perspective, however, the President's options appear easily understandable as the result of short-term feedback processes; analysts of that persuasion have no difficulty in understanding why the President would contradict an established line of policy.[40]

Competition between the analytic and cybernetic paradigms offers an important element of discipline to the foreign policy analyst who must operate under conditions in which data are incomplete and quantification is elusive. It aids him in generating contradictory hypotheses for critical events, each with serious plausibility. In making it less likely that facts will be outrageously warped to fit an established theory or that important information will be ignored, such competition may drive analysis deeper than it would otherwise go. It may also help the analyst with his task of making contingent predictions. What is dangerous to him is not so much the occurrence of an event he considered to be unlikely, but rather the occurrence of an event he did not conceive of, whose possibility he did not take into account. At the same time, the foreign policy analyst must realize that the complexities of decisionmaking overwhelm any theory now available. Neither the analytic nor the cybernetic paradigm has established claim to being the only appropriate basis for foreign policy analysis. Nor, taken together, can they be considered a satisfactory resolution of all the relevant debates in the field of decision theory. The principle of encouraging competition among paradigms must be extended to broader perspectives as well.

THE CONTEXT OF DECISIONMAKING

Though the analytic and cybernetic paradigms provide basic theoretical conceptions of the decision process, they are remote from credible real-world applications. In order to conduct foreign policy analysis, one must integrate specific information on a variety of factors which are thought likely to affect the outcome and which are involved in the decision process but which in a strictly logical-theoretical sense are extraneous to the basic theory of decision. Let us call this overlapping area the context of decisionmaking. Since context is a necessary component of any actual decision process, it belongs in any review aimed at the foreign policy analyst.

Bureaucratic Politics

American scholars have begun to take more serious note of the bureaucratic setting in which foreign policy decisions are always made and its effect on decision outcomes. Neustadt (1960, 1970), Allison (1971), Downs (1967), Halperin and Kantor (1973), Halperin (1974), Hilsman (1967), and Huntington (1961) have been prime expositors of this argument against treating foreign policies as resulting from the decisionmaking process of a unitary, rational (in our terms, aggregated analytic), international actor. Most of their discussions have focused on the generation of

---

[40] See the detailed analysis in Steinbruner (1974).

American foreign policy, though Neustadt also considers the foreign policy behavior of other (Western) governments.

This literature treats the pattern of political relationships which arise between individuals who hold different institutional positions in the machinery of government. Decisionmakers pursue values which are determined more by personal and organizational interests than by an abstract calculus of national interest. They engage in struggles for influence and make elaborate bargaining arrangements which extend over a variety of substantive issues. In such a bureaucratic setting no individual actor is ever completely dominant in the sense that he is unconstrained by the other actors. Outcomes are jointly determined, and, as a result, the overall coherence of the process and the outcomes it generates is far less than one expects to occur from a process determined by generally accepted analytic calculations. Even very important decisions are often by-products of esoteric bureaucratic games.

The general literature on organizations[41] discusses the kinds of values individuals and organizational subunits typically pursue, the maneuvers for power in which they engage, the impact of historical experience on current policy positions, and a variety of internal processes (budgeting, personnel management). All these factors are integrated into the decision process and affect its character.

Analysis of the bureaucratic setting and its impact does require the use of some model of the decision process, and virtually all of the literature to date uses a model or set of assumptions belonging at least loosely to the analytic paradigm. That is, the actors who man the bureaucratic positions and engage in intra-governmental politics are generally assumed to be analytic calculators. Downs (1967) is explicit on the subject. Allison (1971) sharply distinguishes the bureaucratic perspective from a unitary analytic model and discusses a number of factors which structure the minds of bureaucratic actors, but the decision process in which they are assumed to engage remains an analytic variant. The rest of the literature tends to be less explicit.

The literature is replete with studies of specific decisions in which the influence of various factors of the bureaucratic setting is documented.[42] The theoretical coherence of the topic has not been sufficient, however, to allow any powerful empirical generalizations to emerge from the series of case studies.

Sensitivity to the bureaucratic perspective is clearly necessary to the policy analyst, though problematic. One searches through the literature in vain for the description of important decisions in which careful examination revealed that the effects of the bureaucratic setting were insignificant. The analyst can be sure that if he does not know the organizational structure which has or will make a decision he is concerned with and if he does not know the state of affairs within that structure, then his analysis will be extremely crude and possibly quite misleading. This is a burdensome requirement, for the necessary details are often difficult to obtain and the guidelines which emerge from the literature as to what information to look for are not very precise.

Organizational Process

Allison (1971) insists on a distinction between organizational procedure and bureaucratic politics. The latter involves the intentional actions and conscious cal-

---

[41] Blau (1955), Bower (1970), Chandler (1962), Huntington (1961), March (1965), March and Simon (1958), and Thompson (1967).

[42] The number is far too great to review, but good examples are provided in: Armacost (1969), Lowenthal (1972), Sapolsky (1973), Wellford (1973), and Wildavsky (1962). Many of the general works discussed above include case illustrations and some were inspired by case studies.

culations of particular actors; the former refers to the body of largely routine procedure which sets the pattern of activity in any established organization and constitutes a further argument against treating foreign policies as resulting from "unitary rational" international actors. In the case of the Cuban missile crisis which Allison uses to develop his analysis, the location of the U.S. naval blockade appears to have contradicted the intentions and explicit orders of President Kennedy and Secretary of Defense McNamara. The reason, it seems, was related to standard operational procedures of the U.S. Navy which made that organization extremely resistant to conducting naval patrols within range of Cuban air defenses.

The theoretical analysis of organizational routine fits directly within the cybernetic paradigm. There is a large descriptive literature which details the kinds of procedures one finds in various organizations: accounting procedures, work hours, work assignments, seniority rules, promotion criteria, control systems, communications, etc. There is also a large literature[43] on small group processes in organizations which has both strong theoretical and descriptive content. These areas offer important direction and background information to the foreign policy analyst, but they are sufficiently beyond the topic of decisionmaking that they will not be reviewed here.

Promising work which does relate both the structure and process of organizations to theoretical accounts of decisionmaking has been provided by analysts of business decisions. Bower (1970) has studied the resource allocation process within American business organizations and found that it did not correspond to analytic assumptions. He constructs a model of the organizational decision processes which details the roles played by various levels of the organizational hierarchy. He makes it clear that initiative tends to come from low levels in a large organization, that middle managers provide the necessary impetus for those projects which are carried through, and that with respect to decisions about specific organizational activities the highest levels engage in a process of ratification. Aharoni (1966) provides somewhat compatible observations in observing how a number of firms make foreign investment decisions. He supports Bower's assertion that analytic assumptions do not stand up to careful observation, making use of cybernetic assumptions in describing the process he observes.

Everything Else

Once the discussion goes beyond the setting of bureaucratic politics and organizational procedure—which are reasonably well defined in the literature—the context of decisionmaking can include virtually any factor which affects the activity of government. Culture, national style, historical experience, broad economic forces, domestic politics, and international military balances—these phrases all refer vaguely to a range of influences at least some of which will be important in virtually any significant instance of decisionmaking. The obvious problem is that this broad array is virtually guaranteed to swamp any theoretical enterprise which attempts to cope systematically with all of it. This is the problem with the Snyder, Bruch, and Sapin book (1962) which has been a stalwart for those explicitly concerned with foreign policy decisionmaking or a decisionmaking approach to international relations. One must concede, as the book suggests, that the foreign policy decision process indeed is open to a broad range of factors. The attempt to list these factors by broad categories results in a taxonomy; it does not yield a coherent theory of decision.

---

[43] Reviewed in March (1965).

To be sure, a research procedure which correlated specific situational variables with outcomes clearly resulting from specific decisions could provide an implicit theory of decision, or at least systematic evidence which any viable theory of decision would have to incorporate. This possibility has not in fact been actualized. One is left with the truism that aspects of the economic, political, cultural, technological, and historical setting must be incorporated into the analysis of any actual decision process. How that crucial step is taken depends upon the skills of the individual analyst.

SUPPLEMENTARY THEORIES

Portions of the decisionmaking literature cannot be appropriately subsumed under any of the headings already discussed. Two areas in particular—theories of cognitive processing and theories of motivation—provide theoretical treatments of decisionmaking without reaching the level of discussion represented by the analytic and cybernetic paradigms.

Cognitive Theory

Human decisionmakers, according to cognitive theorists, are more complicated than simple cybernetic assumptions suggest, but they process information in a different way than that suggested by the analytic paradigm. The human mind has the inherent capacity, as one of its chief characteristics, to make inductive inferences which summarize the specific information of immediate experience in terms of general images, ideas, propositions, etc. There appear to be systematic ways in which this is done which hold across the staggering diversity of individuals, groups, and cultures. That is, abstracting from the fantastically varied content of human attitudes and beliefs, there are regularities in the way information is processed and stored by the human brain which give rise to some theoretical generalizations about the process of decision. Steinbruner (1974) argues that the principles of cognitive organization can be fruitfully utilized to extend the assumptions of the cybernetic paradigm beyond the simple problems used as prototypes for abstract analysis to the world of complex policy problems—specifically, decisions on sharing nuclear weapons within NATO.

Cognitive psychology is a well developed field which, of course, cannot be reviewed here any more than can microeconomics. As Neisser (1967) makes clear, most of the work has been done under controlled laboratory conditions and remains very far removed from applied decision theory. This area, however, holds out some promise. It is clear that greater sophistication must be built into the theory of decision, and it is reasonable to look to those who have carefully and systematically studied the operations of the human mind for a base from which to proceed.

De Rivera (1968) makes a concerted attempt to mediate between the world of psychology and the world of high politics. His political analysis is not penetrating, but he does state some promising psychological themes: for example, the effect of small group interactions in structuring and stabilizing uncertain judgments and the role of selective mechanisms of perception. Jervis (1968) utilizes some of the literature of cognitive psychology to formulate a number of propositions as to why misperceptions tend to arise in international relations. Abelson (1973) develops a cognitive analysis of political belief structures. Janis (1972) applies well researched propositions about the effects of group interactions on human beliefs to a number of important political events.

Schroeder, Driver, and Streufert (1967) have developed an analysis of information processing operations using political games which represent at least primitive versions of policy problems. This work has used the traditional experimental methods of psychology and thus has established a degree of empirical validity within a laboratory context. The games are far too simple and stylized, however, to represent much of a step beyond the laboratory setting. Also their central cognitive variable—cognitive complexity—is too unrefined to offer a convincing replication of the decision process. Steinbruner (1970) has used somewhat more complicated games to demonstrate the characteristics of cognitive decision processes; again there is the inherent problem of generalizing beyond the laboratory setting.

In bringing to bear a great deal of experimental evidence, the cognitive approach offers a much more solid empirical base than any other approach to decisionmaking. Unfortunately, this base is narrow, and little attention has been paid to the complicated task of extending it beyond the laboratory. Since it does not have as yet the rigorous theoretical base of either the analytic or the cybernetic paradigm, its status at the moment is best described as a promising supplementary theory.

Theories of Personality

The concept of the decision process in the literature reviewed to this point focuses on the processing and integrating of information. It requires conceptions of value which are either articulated directly or mapped onto a set of preferences about the environment, but it does not inquire into the motives which generate the values, and which presumably impel decisionmakers to intervene in the flow of events. There is, of course, a rich literature in psychology which does inquire into human motives, and for current purposes this can properly be considered supplementary to the theory of decision (though most psychologists would probably reverse the relationship).

The dominant figure in this field is still Freud, since he provided the most complete and most usable model of human personality.[44] The most promising recent development of psychoanalytic theory is the work of Erikson (1950, 1959, 1969, 1958, 1962) who, in setting forth a psychosocial impulse instead of the classic psychosexual motives of Freudian theory, seems to have moved closer to the world of politics. Both writers analyze the structure of motives which drive human behavior and uncover pathways which are startling to the conventional mind. Though this has earned them the reputation as theorists of irrational behavior, that results largely from the unusual values which their analysis illuminates. Once one grants him the motives his theory suggests, Freud appears to have no quarrels with the analytic paradigm. The ego, as the mediator between impulses of the id, the moral constraints of the superego, and the reality constraints of the external world, is at least in a loose sense an analytic decisionmaker.

The basic psychoanalytic theory, developed originally to cope with pathological modes of behavior, has been extended to normal human operations and particularly to political decisionmaking by means of a number of different arguments. The most direct of these undertakes a psychoanalytic interpretation of some important political leader using such evidence as is available in the public record. There are recent books of this genre on Kennedy,[45] Nixon,[46] Hitler,[47] and Gandhi.[48] They vary greatly

[44] A brief introduction to Freud can be gleaned from Fenichel (1945), Freud (1946, 1948, 1960), and Hall (1954).

[45] Church (1973).

[46] Mazlish (1972).

[47] Langer (1972).

[48] Erikson (1969).

in quality, but all of them struggle under the fundamental difficulty that the central method—the psychoanalytic interview—is not available. Leaders will not submit to the prolonged and intense examination which Freud required of his patients and upon which his theoretical analysis depends. Operating on an incomplete public record, which the very theory at work expects to be distorted, is inherently problematic. It is a thoroughly tautological procedure without the natural controls which might be provided by a large amount of pertinent information or a competitive theory. Thus there is a great deal of art involved in the procedure and the quality of the work depends considerably on the care and sensitivity of the author. One of the best of these psychological biographies—the interpretation of Woodrow Wilson by George and George (1956)—uses the psychoanalytic framework to structure its analysis, but does not discuss that framework explicitly and integrates the analysis into a large body of the usual historical information. That represents perhaps the best model for this general approach.

There have been more systematic attempts to generalize psychoanalytic theory to the political world. Lasswell (1930) used the basic notion of displacement to provide a general model of political motivation. He derived from it different kinds of political actors—agitators and administrators—which, he asserted, are to be found in the decision process. Lasswell based his analysis on actual interviews of persons in political life, though he had no particular outcome or decision in view and thus stands well to the academic side of the policy analyst. For whatever reasons this lead, which was developed over 40 years ago, has not generated much subsequent research.

There has also been a sophisticated attempt to combine psychoanalytic theory with some of the insights and methods of anthropology in order to construct a coherent analysis of political events with empirical content. The concept of political culture has been developed[49] suggesting that psychoanalytic themes are deposited in a nation's culture and come to affect political decisions through the normal operations of cultural variables. Pye (1962) and Benedict (1946) are particularly good examples of works in which this kind of argument is used to produce an interpretation of the typical political behavior of an entire nation. Again the difficulty for the political analyst is that the approach has not been developed to produce the kind of fine-grained analysis required to analyze and to predict particular outcomes.

There are also analyses of motive forces which do not derive from the psychoanalytic tradition but rather from the large body of experimental work which has been a major subfield in psychology for decades. Gurr (1970) has adopted the well-researched hypothesis that frustration produces aggression to derive an analysis of political behavior. This has not been widely used in analyses of specific decisions, but it is directly applicable and potentially useful. Lorenz (1966) and Ardrey (1966) have provided more exotic and highly speculative arguments based on the analysis of instinctual behavior, particularly in subhuman species.

In general, the analysis of motivational forces clearly is a topic which impinges on decision theory and undoubtedly would be extremely important if the analysis had achieved a high degree of empirical validity. It has not done so, however, nor has it achieved quite the abstract theoretical coherence which exists in analytical decision theory. Insofar as foreign policy analysts may be insensitive to the workings of human motives, it provides ample stimulus to recognize the importance of the topic.

---

[49] Pye and Verba (1965).

CASE STUDIES

The previous discussion has concerned the literature on decisionmaking in general. Part of the literature has focused specifically on crisis conditions, and thus is of obvious relevance to this review. It can be divided into two categories: first, works analyzing the general impact of the crisis situation on decisions and outcomes; and, second, case studies of particular crises.

Crisis in General

Virtually all students of decisionmaking recognize "crisis" as referring to circumstances of decision which have a special character and unusual significance. Although there is no widely accepted definition, the word "crisis" often implies unusual stress on the decisionmakers, unusual priority given to the decision problem, unusually extensive or important consequences accruing from the decision. Events often become possible in a crisis which could not occur under normal conditions (e.g., mobilization of military forces, with the resulting disruption of civilian lives). The balance of large contextual forces is such that the factors controlled by decisionmakers are widely understood to be capable of deflecting the course of historical events. All this is evident to intuitive observers.

Theoretical analysis of the properties of international political crisis has not developed much beyond such intuitive generalizations. One cannot find agreement in the literature, to illustrate, on even such an apparently fundamental point as to whether the density of crises in a particular period leads toward or away from war. McClelland's (1961) review of the topic cites this example, suggesting that the field of international relations had accumulated little established knowledge on the topic and speculating about promising lines of future research. A decade later Hermann (1969a, 1972), reviewing the topic, was still forced to deal with interesting leads and programs for research rather than established analysis. In a recent compendium reviewing the state of scholarship on crisis, James Robinson (in Hermann, 1972) notes that the study of crisis has been only loosely connected to the main theoretical literature on decisionmaking.

Hermann (1969a) does advance interesting suggestions regarding the critical properties of crisis. He argues that a threat to important values, short time sequence, and an element of surprise to decisionmakers are the components of crisis, and that if one element is missing then the situation falls distinctly short of crisis. He advances a scheme for classifying decision problems using all three dimensions. This allows him to define a three-dimensional space and to associate well known historical events with particular points in that space. The result is suggestive for a research program and might well jolt more reflectiveness out of a foreign policy analyst prone to forget or overlook historical evidence.

There have been attempts to simulate crisis decision processes using established theoretical conceptions. Pool and Kessler (1965), for example, present a computer program which simulates the behavior of the Kaiser and the Tsar during the crisis in July of 1914. The program utilizes principles taken from cognitive psychology. Though it attempts to specify how these worked in the crisis, it does not purport to advance a decision process whose basic character is peculiar to the crisis situation. Hermann and Hermann's (1967) simulation of the same 1914 crisis is similar.

In short, there is little danger that the competent analyst will be insensitive to the significance of crisis conditions and little solid generalization which decision theory has to offer as to how precisely the presence of crisis will affect the decision process. "Crisis" denotes another set of contextual elements that the analyst must blend with assumptions of decision theory to get a useful product.

Crisis in Particular

A rich historical literature discusses the events of some of the prominent international crises of the past. This literature contains the basic information against which any analysis of crisis behavior must test its plausibility. The literature is not all that we would wish it to be, for the evidence presented is almost always incomplete in some dimensions; and, since the literature is the work of many hands, it does not as a whole yield systematic knowledge. It constitutes nonetheless the digested, communicable, reflective experience on the topic which our culture has been able to accumulate. The foreign policy analyst concerned with crisis behavior should certainly have a working knowledge of this literature.

It requires particularly precarious judgments to select noteworthy examples from the broad literature. The works mentioned are meant to be illustrative of those in which the authors have done serious, penetrating historical work to establish the facts of a particular crisis. Yet these cases are not treated as wholly unique, but rather as forerunners toward general understanding.

The Wohlstetter Study (1962) of Pearl Harbor

This is a justly famous piece of work which reflects a thorough research of archival materials, Congressional hearings, etc., to reconstruct the sequence of events leading to the Japanese attack on Pearl Harbor. The attack was preceded by a crisis in Japanese-American relations against the backdrop of world crisis associated with World War II. The focus of concern is why the United States failed to anticipate the attack and defend against it; it is in essence a study of a failure of intelligence services. The theoretical analysis emphasizes the problem of extracting genuine signals from background noise and this constitutes an extremely simple but nonetheless provocative use of cybernetic assumptions.

The Whaley Study (1973) of Operation Barbarossa

A recently prepared companion study to the Wohlstetter effort is Whaley's study of Operation Barbarossa—the German invasion of the Soviet Union in 1941. This is another instance in which a critical turn of a major crisis was not effectively anticipated despite, as Whaley documents, the availability of rather extensive information on the fact and the date of the impending attack. Whaley argues that strategic deception rather than mere "noise" was the essential reason why Hitler was able to mislead Stalin, most of the Soviet bureaucracy, and most of the rest of the attending world as well. Soviet decisionmakers were not misled by ambiguity, but rather false certainty. The argument has obvious implications for cognitive analysis.

The Tuchman Study (1962) of the Outbreak of World War I

Tuchman's well known book on the outbreak of World War I is one of the best available studies of crisis behavior. While the study is presented in purely historical terms, her account of the unfolding of the von Schlieffen plan is one of the better documented examples of the impact of established organizational procedure. Similarly, her account of the maneuvers of the German Admiral von Souchan in the Mediterranean as the war broke out and the failure of the Allies to perceive their significance is a classic study of cognitive mechanisms and their impact on decision-making.

The Allison Study (1971) of the Cuban Missile Crisis

In a work which has been repeatedly cited, Allison analyses the events of the Cuban missile crisis from three separate theoretical perspectives: aggregated (Model I, "Rational Actor") and disaggregated (Model II, "Organizational Process" and Model III, "Governmental Politics"). Models I and III embody the analytic paradigm; Model II is developed from assumptions in the cybernetic paradigm. Although emphasizing U.S. actions, he demonstrates that the separate perspectives illuminate very different aspects of the crisis, and that behavior which appears anomalous from one perspective is perfectly understandable from another.

The Neustadt Study (1970) of Suez and Skybolt

Neustadt analyzes and compares two crises in British-American relationships over the Suez Canal in 1956 and the Skybolt missile in 1962. He finds that in each case the two governments badly misunderstood each other because each failed to penetrate the internal politics of the other. Since these were two unusually close allies sharing language and political heritage, there is a presumption *a fortiori* that this kind of problem is even more significant in other contexts. The study suggests a systematic failure in intelligence assessment and diplomatic reporting which is certainly not contradicted by the other studies.

The Williamson Study (1969) of 1914

Williamson has traced the impact of military planning and of the organizational postures thereby established on the unfolding of the 1914 crisis. He examines the British-French military discussions which preceded World War I and which generated the plans, policy concepts, and bureaucratic arrangements which in the actual crisis sent the British into the war on the side of France. The study demonstrates that the crisis decisions were powerfully conditioned by the internal bureaucratic situation within the two governments. The book also documents the central role played by General (and later Field Marshal) Henry Wilson, an extremely interesting subject for cognitive analysis.

The Paige Study (1968) of Korea

Glenn Paige's study of the United States decison to intervene in Korea is structured in terms of the framework for analysis of decisionmaking advanced by Snyder, Bruck, and Sapin (1962). Paige's study relates the conditions of crisis to the broad range of variables suggested by that framework. The result is an extended list of propositions about behavior of decisionmakers and their institutions, each illustrated by the Korean case.

Unfortunately, propositions are not related to available theoretical models of the decision process. They stand rather awkwardly as simple, non-quantitatively stated empirical generalizations which make broader assertions than the Korean case alone will bear, but are not supported by a general theoretical structure. Thus the book presents a network of "variables" with the sign of some of their relationships indicated: e.g., "The greater the crisis, the greater the environmental demands for response information" (assertion of a positive relationship) and "the greater the crisis, the less the international acceptability of information about it emanating from the decisionmakers directly concerned" (assertion of a negative relationship) (p. 312). Such an enterprise stands much closer to generalized description than to theoretical analysis.

RECAPITULATION

A number of conclusions emerge from this review of the literature on decision-making:

1. *An examination of government decisionmaking systems under crisis conditions reveals that decisionmakers chronically and seriously misestimate the flow of events, particularly the behavior of other governments.* This is not only the expected failure to predict exact events but also a failure to understand underlying influences. This observation is compellingly demonstrated by the small number of case studies reviewed; it is supported in the broader literature.

2. *There is no theory of decision to be found in the social sciences with established empirical validity across the range of events one must include in the category crisis decisionmaking.* Empirical models have demonstrated partial success with respect to very limited types of decisions, and this is significant. There is at the moment and for the foreseeable future, however, no model which will provide comprehensive, consistent explanations or accurate, reliable predictions based on quantitative calculations for the range of decisions which must concern the policymaker. Indeed, the state of the art is so far from such an ideal and its hypothetical achievement so questionable on philosophical grounds that it is an inappropriate criterion against which to judge the utility of theoretical work in this area.

3. *Significant benefits can accrue to the foreign policy analyst if he can generate multiple perspectives on the phenomena he examines.* Such pluralism can help him produce better alternative explanations and contingent predictions. It can sensitize the analyst to the fact that no single approach can adequately capture the essential features of most complex problems. More attention to alternative approaches, both at the level of "models" and accompanying contextual factors and their underlying paradigms is justified.

4. *The quality of analysis will depend directly upon the analyst's knowledge of, inter alia, organizational and bureaucratic context.* The historical record makes abundantly clear that major decisions and the outcomes generated are always affected by the bureaucratic and organizational setting in which they occur. It is reasonable to treat information on the internal structure of a government as a data requirement for all theories of decision purporting to explain or predict its behavior under crisis. If such information is lacking, that fact constitutes a sharp warning to the analyst and imposes a high probability of error on his estimates.

5. *Both the analytic and the cybernetic paradigms provide a coherent structure of logic useful for disciplining explanations and contingent predictions which must be made on an imprecise basis.* These paradigms and the more detailed models which they generate can serve to improve the judgment of the foreign policy analyst. They may help reinforce or correct his intuitive calculations and connect them more rigorously to that body of hard evidence which does exist.

6. *Either of the two base paradigms can be used to structure explanations and predictions under conditions where the data base is severely restricted.* The analytic paradigm has a distinct advantage deriving from its greater development and general familiarity. To the extent that the cybernetic paradigm drives the analyst to greater disaggregation of the decisionmaking unit than does the standard unitary rational actor mode of the analytical paradigm, its data requirements are considerably more demanding; however, where the level of disaggregation is comparable, the differing logical structures of the two paradigms do not appear to pose drastically different data requirements.

7. *The analytic and cybernetic paradigms are unevenly developed at the moment.* The structure of analytic decision theory is far more articulated and greater

effort has been devoted to working out its implications for actual policy problems. The professional training of those concerned with policy questions has been suffused to a greater extent with analytic assumptions. This, it appears, is the result of far greater investment in analytic decision models over a greater number of years. More attention to the cybernetic paradigm appears to be warranted.

8. *The supplementary theories involving cognitive operations and motivational forces do seem to require more detailed information to be useful.* Of these, cognitive theory presents the more tractable problem. Conclusions can probably be drawn on the basis of simple, reasonably available information contained in speeches, newspaper articles, individual biographies, and basic facts of organizational structure. Theories of motivation require more esoteric and demanding information, and for their most valid application they require direct and extensive access to specific individuals under special interview conditions.

9. *Decision theory can enrich, not replace, the analyst's capacity for judgment.* More attention to methodological issues such as those raised here can give the foreign policy analyst useful new perspectives on his subject matter. This can increase the knowledge, skills, capacity for judgment, and intuition which remain central to his art.

Decision theory is not, in short, a science. Its elegant and stimulating theories do not connect solidly enough to empirical measurements to allow the sound basis for prediction which the natural and physical sciences afford. That does not mean the theory is not useful and important, however. Care taken in structuring assumptions and deriving coherent arguments from them will presumably improve the quality of policy analysis, including foreign policy analysis. Examination of foreign policy decisionmaking is inevitably an exercise in piecing together inadequate evidence to form a reasonably coherent picture. Decision theory offers a body of argument and limited but rigorous evidence that serve to establish which pictures of reality in general are plausible and which are not. It enables the informed analyst to take some pieces of evidence more seriously than he otherwise would and draw from them more systematic implications. That does not guarantee against error. It does seem to promise at least a marginal improvement in performance. But, if it is to benefit the analyst of Soviet foreign policy, the theory must first be applied to the Soviet context.

III. DECISION-THEORY-RELATED APPROACHES TO THE STUDY OF SOVIET FOREIGN POLICY

EVOLUTION OF SOVIET STUDIES

Academic studies of Communist affairs, including Soviet foreign policy, are in a period of uncertain transition. For almost two decades after World War II, most of the academic literature embodied the "area studies" approach. With the post-war emergence of the United States and the Soviet Union as the two major world powers, "area studies," funded heavily by the U.S. Government and private foundations, were vigorously promoted in order to reduce the American "knowledge gap" about the Soviet Union.

Launched as a crash effort to raise understanding of the Soviet political system to the level of knowledge about more familiar Western systems, the area focus of Soviet studies was narrowed by other considerations. While many pioneers in the field of Soviet studies had broad academic backgrounds, scholars of the second and succeeding generations often devoted themselves exclusively to the area. At their best, area studies required broad multidisciplinary training and immersion in the history, languages, and culture of a particular region that left little time for major substantive concern with non-area societies or for specialization in the methods and techniques of a single discipline. Teaching and research drew heavily on the work of émigrés who devoted themselves exclusively to analysis of Communist affairs. Paucity of basic information about the Soviet system required students of Soviet affairs to devote disproportionate time and energy to reconstructing or estimating data taken as "given" in the study of Western societies—gross economic indicators and information about the formal structure and functions of party and government institutions, for example. Dependence for data on a narrow range of tightly controlled official Soviet published materials compelled students of Soviet affairs to concentrate on developing techniques especially tailored to that distinctive data base, e.g., deciphering "esoteric communications" among members of the Soviet (and foreign Communist) elites. Given the formal institutional, ethnocentric approach to the study of foreign political systems then dominating American political science, the evident uniqueness of the Soviet system under Stalin provided little incentive for students of Soviet affairs to look beyond their area focus.

Academic studies of Soviet foreign policy during this period typically treated the USSR as a unitary international actor motivated by unique, cultural-Russian or, alternatively, ideological-Bolshevik impulses. Examples are Kulski (1959) and Kennan (1961).[50] This dominant approach was complemented by analyses from the "Kremlinological school," which considered the impact of factional conflict within the top Soviet leadership on policy issues (more often domestic than foreign).[51] Indeed in the Soviet context, "Kremlinology" may be regarded as an intellectual antecedent of the "bureaucratic politics" approach to the study of foreign policy.

Soviet area studies developed in the United States at roughly the same time as the "behavioral revolution" transformed traditional American political science. One Sovietologist has characterized this departure from traditionalism as:

---

[50] For categorizations and illustrations of some of these imputed impulses, see Reshetar (1955), and Bell (1958).

[51] A classic is Conquest (1961).

a concentration on both the observable political actions of individuals and groups and the psychological processes which influence these actions—e.g., perceptions, motives, and attitudes. The expected end result will be the identification of uniformities in political behavior that can be expressed in generalizations or theories with explanatory or predictive power. In order to accomplish this, rigorous research techniques should be employed in the collection of data; generalizations must be stated in such a way that they can be tested against empirical data; and, as far as possible, quantifiable data should be employed.[52]

The large body of research spawned by behavioralism and related tendencies was marred by twin excesses of grand theorizing—building constructs unrelatable to the real world—and "inputism"—the collection of whatever data was readily available with little regard for its political relevance.[53] But the behaviorists also generated an innovative body of empirical analyses of non-Communist political systems, as expressed in the work of Almond, Apter, Coleman, Deutsch, Eckstein, and others.

Only in the mid-1960s did the "behavioral revolution" begin to be echoed in the field of Soviet studies, particularly among younger Soviet specialists who argued that the isolation of Soviet studies from the general discipline of political science had become counterproductive. Injunctions to link the field of Soviet studies more systematically with the "mainstream of political science" fueled broad reappraisals of the general state of Soviet studies. Other developments, too, contributed to this stock-taking and self-critical movement. A number of scholars confessed to a sense of déjà vu; as one asserted, "Our arguments were becoming repetitious to the point of utter tedium."[54] Others feared that traditional modes of analysis tailored to the study of the Stalinist system were no longer appropriate, either because of changes in the Soviet system itself or because they rested on inherently faulty assumptions about the uniqueness of the Soviet system, the attributes of the "totalitarian model," the relationship between ideological content and aggressive behavior abroad, etc.[55] Rebelling against both the professional and intellectual isolation engendered by continued treatment of the USSR as *sui generis*, scholars argued for the creation of broader alternative conceptual frameworks, e.g., the Soviet Union as one of a class of Communist-ruled states, of rapidly industrializing societies, of bureaucratically governed polities, or of major actors in an international system or subsystem. This reversion against focusing on the uniqueness of the Soviet system unfortunately occurred before much progress had been made in the systematic building of pre-theories specific to the study of the Soviet Union. Theory-building efforts thus leap-frogged that stage and focused on the search for theoretical frameworks that could encompass more inclusive, if not universal phenomena.

This reappraisal has given rise, particularly during the past half decade, to a number of efforts, many explicitly provisional and experimental, to develop alternative approaches to the study of the Soviet Union by drawing on contemporary social science concepts, theories, and techniques. The main vehicle for this effort to integrate Soviet studies into the social science mainstream has been through comparative Communist studies, which aim at promoting the development of theory and empirical studies concerning the general characteristics of Communist-ruled polities, as well as the factors that distinguish them from each other and from non-Communist systems. Although a lively discussion of theoretical and methodological

[52] Kanet (1971), p. 2.

[53] *Ibid*, p. 3.

[54] Rigby (1970), p. 2.

[55] See the discussion in Blackmer (1968).

issues was launched toward the end of the 1960s[56] as yet few empirical studies embodying comparative approaches of the relevant disciplines have appeared.

Foreign policy studies of the Soviet Union and other Communist states, however, have been little affected by these new stirrings. Both the extensive literature about the comparative study of Communist systems and the small body of empirical research it has inspired are oriented overwhelmingly toward the domestic politics of the Soviet Union and other Communist states.[57] This preoccupation with internal behavior reflects the major foci of comparative political theory. Moreover, comparative studies of Communist foreign policies have been retarded by the long prevailing view that the external behavior at least of the East European Communist-ruled states is strongly controlled by the Soviet Union (i.e., that the foreign policies of Warsaw Pact states are monolithic). A major exception is the area of Sino-Soviet relations, which have been widely studied, but rarely in the context of a broad theoretical framework derived from the general field of international relations or comparative politics.

The literature on Soviet foreign policy continues therefore to be overwhelmingly traditional, historical-descriptive, in character. Broad propositions about Soviet foreign policy behavior are advanced in this literature intermittently, but not systematically. The field continues to be marked by great diversity, both with respect to basic assumptions and content. There is little cumulation of comparable propositions and hypotheses. A systematic inventory of such propositions and hypotheses remains to be compiled, although Welch (1970) has classified major representative works in the field during the 1960s according to a scale of "images" of the Soviet Union ranging from "ultra-hard" to "ultra-soft." In another survey of the state of the field, Welch and Triska (1971) found a paucity of Soviet foreign policy studies that could be classified as "analytical," according to even the loosest usage of that term.

Although only a small portion of the Soviet foreign policy literature contains a self-conscious and reasonably systematic effort to employ an explicit theoretical framework, a growing number of scholars of Soviet foreign policy have begun to introduce *techniques* of contemporary social science into their research (e.g., multivariate analysis, quantitative content analysis), but for the most part on an ad hoc and often on a frankly experimental basis, without particular reference to any overarching theoretical or conceptual framework. Even less of this work has been informed by the developments in decision theory surveyed in Sec. II. Reasons for this gap and an assessment of the potential utility of decision-theory-related approaches to the study of Soviet foreign policy will be discussed later. But to provide some understanding of the intellectual setting of the field and the relevance of work done to date for decision-related approaches, we first review briefly some of the recent efforts in the study of Soviet foreign policy to incorporate methods and techniques of contemporary social science.

INNOVATIVE STUDIES OF SOVIET FOREIGN POLICY

The most substantial and ambitious effort in innovative Sovietology is the Tris-

---

[56] See Skilling (1960), Tucker (1967a), and the *Newsletter on Comparative Studies of Communism,* issued periodically between 1968 and 1973 by the Planning Group on Comparative Communist studies of the American Council of Learned Societies.

[57] Gati, *et al.* (1971) have noted this and urged more attention to comparative study of Communist foreign policy.

ka and Finley (1968) textbook on Soviet foreign policy. Frankly experimental, it is an eclectic effort to demonstrate that "new techniques of political analysis show some prospect for allowing more precise handling of data in a field still relegated by many to the occult arts" (p. xiii). The study is a mixture of historical-descriptive material, conventional analysis of Soviet foreign policymaking institutions and the educational and career backgrounds of leading political figures, quantitative content analysis to measure the frequency and, by inference, importance of doctrinally stereotyped words or phrases in the public utterances of these leaders, and formulation of an "actional-symmetry construct"—derived from criminal law and the law of torts—as a basis for a quantitative measure of Soviet risk-taking propensities in post-war international crises.

The Triska/Finley approach to the study of Soviet foreign policymaking institutions falls squarely into the framework of the aggregated analytical paradigm, termed by them the "synoptic model": "a self-maintaining system must preserve a synoptically rational decision process" (p. 69). It is acknowledged that this process is mediated in practice by the personal backgrounds and group affiliations of individual decisionmakers, their shared and individually distinctive belief systems, and by the differential impacts of events; but the study provides no integrated theory or modeling of the interaction of these variables and no criteria for weighing their respective values.

For purposes of this review, the model of Soviet risk-taking propensities developed by Triska and Finley (Chapter 9) is the most useful test for gauging the empirical value of their approach. The methodology is complex, consisting of the superimposition of crisis typologies and Soviet crisis moves, the ranking of crises according to a scale of intensity, the elaboration of coefficients of inherent riskiness, and a scaling of "bids" or action moves of the adversaries.

Findings are expressed in generalizations of the following order: "[The] level and pattern of Soviet risk assumed in the twenty-nine crises [examined] have been *low* and *narrow*. Soviet crisis behavior was found to be conservative rather than radical, cautious rather than reckless, deliberate rather than impulsive, and rational (not willing to lose) rather than nonrational" (p. 346). Selected examples of the more detailed conclusions: initial Soviet reactions in a crisis ("bidding") were characterized by a mixed pattern, with a tendency for higher bids to be associated with smaller risks; Soviet crisis output varied over time, with risk-avoidance prominent in the immediate post-war period and again in the Khrushchev era; Soviet decisionmakers have been willing to take higher risks vis-à-vis Communist than Western or Third World countries.

Conclusions of the sort, if validated, could provide a degree of empirical confirmation for the "conventional wisdom" about Soviet risk-taking propensities up to the early 1960s. They apply to crises only up to that time and therefore do not take into account either the 1964 change in leadership or the USSR's achievement of nuclear parity and emergence as a globally mobile conventional military power. As tools of explanation and prediction, however, the "overall formulas" of Soviet risk-taking derived from the study and expressed at very high levels of generality in broad tendency terms,[58] have little to offer the foreign policy analyst attempting to anticipate particular kinds of Soviet behavior in particular circumstances.

[58] Examples: "The less concerned with the crisis objective, the lower the Soviet risk-taking propensity ... whereas conversely, the greater the Soviet concern, the less cautious the USSR." "The riskier (the more serious) the crisis, the more cautious the USSR." "The stronger the other party in crisis, the greater the geographical distance from the USSR; and the greater the stakes involved, the more cautious the Soviet crisis response." "The less the Soviet control in 'the socialist system,' the greater the intensity of crisis there." "The more actively a Soviet decision invokes the change in the *status quo* and is directed against normal, routine expectations, the longer the time period to make that decision" (pp. 346-49).

Apart from the issue of the utility of such generalizations to the practitioner and the appropriateness of the "actional-symmetry" model for explaining or predicting Soviet crises behavior, the validity of the Triska/Finley findings depends entirely on the validity of the quantitative values assigned by the authors to the large numbers of qualitative variables employed by the model and fed into the computers (e.g., numerical scaling of crisis intensities and perceptions of stakes). Subjective judgments must also be employed to fill in even ostensibly "objective" data categories.[59] Unfortunately, the case study literature (discussed later) is too thin and heterogeneous to provide the relevant data across a sufficiently broad range of cases from secondary sources. The evidence and arguments adduced by Triska and Finley to support their choice of numerical values and assignments to categories are not displayed.

Similar problems arise in a related study by Schwartz (1967), who attempts to refine the theory of deterrence developed by Schelling and others to make it more applicable to understanding Soviet crisis decisionmaking. Schwartz, too, treats the USSR as a unitary analytic decisionmaker. He seeks to determine covariance between two or more Soviet "objective" and "perceptual" variables (both measured through quantitative content analysis) involved in Soviet crisis decisions that signify deterrence from an American perspective. The study formulates sixteen hypotheses derived from deterrence theory and attempts to test them in past crisis situations. Examples of purportedly confirmed hypotheses: "Where the Soviet Union's foreign policy decisionmakers perceive clear overall U.S. strategic superiority, crisis-limiting actions by the Soviet Union or its allies are associated with increased felt-threat to those decisionmakers" (p. 479). "As U.S. strategic and/or tactical preparedness is perceived by the Soviets to increase, Soviet perceptions of the resolve of U.S. decisionmakers increase" (p. 483). An example of a "disconfirmed" hypothesis: "As threat increases, centralization of decisionmaking increases" (p. 488).

Like the outputs of the Triska/Finley model, the findings of Schwartz's analysis, pitched at a very high level of generality, are of doubtful utility for the foreign policy analyst. Again, the criteria employed for "scoring" the critical perceptual variables manipulated in the model are not displayed.[60] There is no discussion of assumptions about the relationship between the press materials utilized and the crisis perceptions of U.S. and Soviet decisionmakers; there is apparently no allowance for distortion of the perceptual content of these materials as a function of crisis communication strategy (signaling).

Heldman's (1971) study of Soviet policy toward African states examines over time the relationship among four variables: (1) closeness of Soviet and African voting in the United Nations; (2) closeness of bilateral relations; (3) influence of Communist-oriented "progressive" groups in individual African countries; and (4) Soviet perceptions of that influence. Establishing rough quantitative measures for the variables, Heldman finds a statistically meaningful correlation among all four, the highest between (3) and (4) and the lowest between (1) and (3). These conclusions appear to be a confirmation of conventional wisdom and, as such, may enhance the foreign policy analyst's confidence in his implicit assumptions. In this case as generally, however, the exceptions may be of greater interest to the practitioner than the rule.

[59] Including the questionable one behind the identification of the USSR as "initiator" in the 1947 Greek Civil War crisis.

[60] "Guideline indices" were constructed by two to six coders for each variable from examination of foreign and U.S. press materials and reviewed for "inter-coder agreement."

For example, in the case of Madagascar, Heldman found no meaningful correlation between variables (2) and (4).

These three studies, which fit broadly into the framework of the aggregated analytic paradigm, seek to contribute to the creation of theory by establishing relationships between quantified policy inputs and outputs. But Aspaturian (1971), who incorporates the same aggregated analytic paradigm assumptions and input-output perspective, argues that, since the search for quantifiable relationships is illusory, Soviet scholars should settle for a less systematic framework:

> A loose framework that assumes incomplete information, inaccessibility to decisionmakers, and inability to replicate and objectively verify results, and thus explicitly requiring a judgmental component involving informed speculation about hidden or inaccessible data, remains a better vehicle for understanding past, current, and future Soviet foreign policy behavior, than frameworks and models that rely solely upon the manipulation of "hard data" and visible variables (p. 55).

Aspaturian proposes one such loose framework, consisting of five "variables": (1) Motivations/Purposes/Intentions; (2) Capabilities/Power; (3) Risks; (4) Costs/Benefits; and (5) Opportunities. The variables are subdivided into "voluntaristic" and "deterministic" ones; checklists are provided for components of each variable.

Aspaturian makes only modest claims for this loose framework. It is offered not as a device for prediction but to "provide a basis for explaining past and current Soviet foreign policy and to understand and analyze future behavior as it occurs." It is also intended explicitly as an antidote to frameworks relying solely on quantitative techniques, "to demonstrate the inseparability of voluntaristic and objective factors involved in the shaping of Soviet foreign policy and the distortions that would result if quantifiable factors and inputs alone were calculated." However, neither Aspaturian nor any other scholar has attempted to apply a loose framework of this kind. It is doubtful that it can be operationalized beyond the checklists already provided which at best may suggest to the practicing analyst "something he hadn't thought of" in reaching a judgment about a particular policy issue.

Two additional subcategories of innovative Sovietology in the aggregated analytic tradition may be distinguished: game-theoretical and international-system studies. Welsh (1969) examines Soviet and American behavior in the Hungarian crisis of 1956, utilizing an axiomatic, game-theoretical framework inspired by Schelling (the only example in the literature of this approach). A set of categories derived from game theory is manipulated to "predict" rational behavior; observed real-world actions are then compared to that prediction. Postulating explicit assumptions concerning mutual perception of intentions, Welsh concludes that the "model" accurately "predicted" the Soviet intervention (but not U.S. behavior).

Welsh cautions that his frankly experimental piece has no predictive value, claiming for it at most a contribution to partial descriptive theory. Even with this caveat, Welsh's heuristic and analogical use of game theory has no discernible application as "descriptive theory" to the work of the foreign policy analyst. The value of the approach, rather, lies in two techniques which it incorporates: formulation of a "payoff matrix" as an explicit table of Soviet and American policy preferences and explicit consideration of sequential Soviet-American interaction.

Even further removed from decision theory is the international systems approach, applied by scholars to the study of Soviet foreign policy. Optimally, the approach allows one to "focus upon the actions of nations as the components of the [international] system; upon the structure and functioning of the system which results from the interaction of nations; or upon the environmental factors which condition both the actions of nations and the operation of the system.[61]

Such an approach is employed in Triska and Finley's analysis (1968, Chapters 5, 8) of the world Communist system, which specifies variables presumed to affect relations among Communist states and provides quantitative as well as qualitative measures. Examples of quantitative indicators are gross national products, natural resources, and degree of urbanization. Several asymmetries among states in the Communist subsystem are identified, but no effort is made to find correlations among the relevant variables, and therefore no generalizations relevant to the foreign policies of the Communist states are presented. Judged in terms of its utility to the practitioner as a conceptual aid, the approach adds nothing to the intuitive generalization that Communist states have something in common, yet differ among themselves in different ways.[62]

Triska and Finley (1968, Chapter 8) also develop a normative interaction model of Soviet-American relations in crisis situations. Soviet-American relations can, they suggest, usefully be conceptualized as a "multiple symmetry" conflict model. They conclude that "unilateral initiation of a novel course of action which effectively unbalances the conflict between antagonists, novel either in nature or magnitude, must elicit a compensating response from the target if the system of which the opponents are part is to recover its previous equilibrium" (p. 298). A proffered example of this finding is the U.S. Government's establishment of the CIA, as a reaction to the KGB. Their conclusions lead to policy prescriptions for the U.S. Government, which may be summarized as: respond in kind ("hard deterrence") while simultaneously attempting to change the ground rules of conflict between the U.S. and the USSR ("peaceful accommodation"). The model has no discernible utility for either explanation or prediction. Its conceptual value is dubious. By definition, a failure of one side to respond (more or less) in kind will tend to induce systemic instability; the character and intensity of the resulting instability are not susceptible to analysis by employment of the model.

Hopmann (1967) treats Communist states as members of an international subsystem in order to examine the degree of cohesion among them in crisis periods. Employing quantitative content analysis of press materials, he seeks to measure attitudes in nine Communist countries toward the United States during four different crisis periods between 1950 and 1965. He concludes that his first hypothesis, "The greater the intersystem conflict, the greater the intrasystem cohesion," is confirmed, but only with respect to a specific "enemy," the United States. This applies equally to the more recent crises, thus partially disproving the second hypothesis: "The more bipolar the international system and the more dominant international cleavages reinforce one another along bipolar lines, the greater the attitudinal consensus among the members of both alliances" (pp. 335-36). The technique employed in the work is so questionable[63] that appraisal of the utility of its conclusions would be superfluous.

Galtung (1966) also treats the Soviet bloc as an international subsystem and examines the extent to which inter-bloc interaction is dependent on the status of a state within that subsystem, and how the interbloc level of conflict affects the pattern of interaction. He concludes that inter-bloc diplomatic and economic relations follow his expected pattern: interaction decreases as the "status" of a state

---

[61] Rosenau (1969), p. 71.

[62] Related products of the Stanford Studies in the Communist System are contained in Triska, ed. (1969).

[63] Hopmann (who limited his analysis to *one* statement by each of eleven governments in four crises).

within the Soviet bloc decreases. The expected pattern was confirmed in part for political and cultural relations; it was disconfirmed for travel. A similar but more rigorous approach, focusing on the Soviet Union's allies and clients, is employed in subsequent studies by Hughes and Volgy (1970) and by Kintner and Klaiber (1971). While the data bases of these studies are narrow, they appear to validate their hypotheses sufficiently to make the conclusions of interest to the foreign policy analyst (e.g., Kintner and Klaiber's point that greater cultural interaction with the West on the part of an East European state does not necessarily signify greater friction with the USSR).

THE CONTEXT OF SOVIET DECISIONMAKING

Bureaucratic Politics

Studies of the Soviet Union as a unitary "Communist" international actor have been complemented by works viewing Soviet foreign policy as one arena in an unending struggle for power among the Soviet leaders. Classical Kremlinology is the study of this "war of all against all," conducted primarily by deciphering esoteric communications within the Soviet leadership. In contrast to the "totalitarian" approach to Soviet politics, which often underlay the unitary actor perspective, the Kremlinological approach assumed that the Leninist party, having formally banned factions and elevated "democratic centralism" to a cardinal principle, did not thereby end internecine conflict but drove it underground. The protagonists had to battle clandestinely without explicitly violating the facade of party unity on which their common political legitimacy rested. This "conflict model" of Soviet elite politics granted that, during the Stalinist terror, the struggle concerned the fruits of secondary power, i.e., access to and influence under the dictator. Prior to Stalin's consolidation of power and after his death, however, the object of struggle was supreme political power in the USSR.

Kremlinology had numerous precedents in studies of court politics, from Byzantium to the Medici. Resting on assumptions implicit in the disaggregated analytic paradigm, it was an intellectual antecedent of the "bureaucratic politics" approach. Classical Kremlinology assumed that political struggle was rarefied; the impact of political institutions and social forces on the struggle for power at the top was marginal.[64]

The power struggle was emphasized over policy conflict. Granting that the latter could assume a life of its own, Kremlinology typically assumed that policy positions were merely symbols for essentially *ad hominem* conflicts about political power. It sometimes further assumed that a victorious leader might reverse policies he had previously espoused in order to reduce his dependence on former political allies. Hence the assumption that factions and patronage *(shefstvo)* should be the central objects of analysis.

Classics of Kremlinology devoting attention to foreign policy include Nicolaevsky (1953) on the Beria affair and Soviet policy in East Germany; Borkenau (1953)

---

[64] In defense of Kremlinology, it should be noted that (at its best) Kremlinology *consciously* minimized the role of institutions and broad social forces on political decisionmaking. Conquest (1961), for example, maintains that "in Soviet circumstances, [large-scale social forces] are not given any direct political expression; they figure simply as influences, competing with other and often more powerful influences, on the moves made in the only area where political change is possible—the central group of politicians" (p. 6).

on Zhdanov's forward policy in the early post-war years; Conquest (1961) on a series of issues between 1953 and 1960 including rapprochement with Yugoslavia. Foreign policy issues are also touched upon in Rush (1958). These studies deal with leadership conflict in narrow terms; there are no successful attempts to deanthropomorphize that conflict by relating it to broader groupings within the political elite.[65]

A number of studies published since the mid-1960s employ a broadened Kremlinological approach. The object and techniques of inquiry have not changed significantly. Ploss (1967) argues, for example, that given the amorphous nature of political interest groupings and internal political divisions within Soviet institutions, "the analyst may best ground his pertinent speculations on a detailed comparison of the differential verbal behavior and prominence of Soviet political personalities." Basing his study of the Khrushchev era on this assumption, Linden (1966) skillfully applies a "conflict model" of Soviet elite politics. Challenging the tendency of the totalitarian concept "to discount the importance of a dualistic or multiplistic politics within the regime itself," Linden argues that "especially in the absence of a terror-imposed discipline in the leadership, the opposing tendencies toward oligarchy and dictatorship remained in constant interplay throughout the Khrushchev era." He explains the dynamic character of politics in the Khrushchev era by the unstable power constellation within the top leadership.[66] In contrast to early Kremlinology, however, Linden gives more weight to the importance of policy disputes *per se.* Although largely devoted to domestic issues, Linden's study relates aspects of Soviet foreign policy, notably Soviet policy toward China and Yugoslavia in 1961-1963, to top-level political struggle.[67]

Most Kremlinological treatments of Soviet foreign policy do not explicitly address the relationship between elite conflict and the "unitary actor" approach. An exception is Armstrong (1965), who suggests that the two approaches are reconcilable through periodization. Leaders manipulate foreign policy issues in the short run; this may even involve marginal sacrifice of "Soviet interests." Yet, "in the *longer run,* any victorious contestant tends to take the position which is consonant with a rational calculation of Soviet interests." This explanation begs the issues of what is "rational" in this context or what differentiates the long from the short run.

More satisfactory is the extensive, explicit case treatment of this issue by Pendill (1969), who examines Soviet policy toward the underdeveloped world between 1952 and 1956. Pendill's research hypothesis was that Soviet policy toward underdeveloped countries was "strongly" influenced by factional differences among Soviet leaders. The hypothesis is substantiated "only in part." Beria and his political allies apparently did reshape Soviet policy toward Iran in 1953 (leading to adoption of a pro-Mossadegh and Tudeh as opposed to a simply anti-Shah policy), as well as in East Germany (where Beria promoted domestic liberalization and rapprochement with West Germany). Such episodes notwithstanding, Soviet policy was, in Pendill's

---

[65] Pethybridge (1962) professed to do this with primary reference to Soviet domestic politics by employing an "interest group" approach, but the empirical parts of his study are limited to analysis of Khrushchev's *personal* conflict with other top Soviet leaders. Useful discussions of the Kremlinological approach are Ploss (1971), Fleron (1969), "Kremlinology" (1964), Linden (1966), and Conquest (1961).

[66] The 1964 ouster of Khrushchev is more satisfactorily explained and was more easily anticipated by the "conflict model" employed by Linden, Leonhard (1963) and others than by the "consolidated succession model" proposed by Lowenthal (1960) and others in a series of articles in *Problems of Communism* between 1960 and 1964. See especially "How Strong is Khrushchev" (1963). The "conflict model" has also been applied to other consolidated Leninist Parties. Nathan (1973) discusses a "factionalism model" of CCP politics; Johnson (1970) applies the approach to domestic and foreign policymaking in the Polish United Workers' Party.

[67] For example, Linden explains oscillations in Soviet policy toward Yugoslavia in 1962 primarily in terms of conflict between Khrushchev and Kozlov; Griffith (1964) explains the same phenomena as resulting from the interaction of Soviet, Chinese, and Yugoslav unitary actors.

analysis, generally formulated "collectively" until 1955. Malenkov and Molotov, who were most directly involved, may have had different motivations, but they evidently agreed on the desirability of enlarging Soviet influence in the Third World through careful, gradual expansion.

However, in 1955-1956, Pendill argues, factional differences had more substantial impact on Soviet foreign policy. Khrushchev, joined by Shepilov, fomented strong anti-Western propaganda campaigns in the Third World (such as one in March 1955) to discredit Malenkov; these campaigns coincided with the periods of greatest instability among the Soviet leaders. Thereafter Khrushchev took over and promoted energetically Malenkov's policy of careful expansion of ties with the Third World in order to buttress his domestic political position against Molotov. For the entire 1952-1956 period, "collective" foreign policies predominated; "these could be expected to be more deliberate, cautious, and open to rational influence, from within the decisionmaking body as well as from without" (p. 75). Pendill's assertion that routine foreign policy organizational processes tend in these circumstances to play a more determining role is plausible, but not documented.

Even in its broadened version, the Kremlinological approach has been criticized as inadequate. Endorsing a "conflict model" of Soviet politics, the critics have urged that more research attention be paid to broader constituencies and wellsprings of policy positions adopted by individuals in the top leadership—on the one hand, interest groupings and institutions; on the other hand, new social forces. Advocates of this "interest group" approach generally assume that political power is pyramidally distributed in the USSR; the Politburo dominates the decisionmaking process far more than the executive or government in a Western political system. "Linkages" between the Politburo and broader policy referents, however, are viewed as more direct than in the past. Concern with *institutions* parallels the "bureaucratic politics" approach to the study of decisionmaking in Washington; concern with elite groupings and broader forces assumes that "crypto-politics" in the Soviet Union, while still greatly constrained by the hierarchical political system (with its key attributes of formal unity and democratic centralism) nonetheless have greater scope than in the past.

These concerns have inspired the development of an exploratory theoretical literature on interest groupings in the Soviet context. The literature is marred by terminological debates and an exchange of charges that, on the one hand, "interest groups" as defined by David Truman and others in the American context are inapplicable to the Soviet Union and, on the other hand, that a handful of leaders alone cannot resolve all political issues in a large country. Between these extreme positions, however, a number of scholars, such as Skilling and Griffiths (1971), have attempted to select elements of Western interest group theory that can improve understanding of Soviet politics and to delineate crypto-organizational forms through which partial "interests" are espoused in the Soviet context.[68]

At present, however, the "interest group" approach has been employed empirically in only a few cases—almost all of them involving internal Soviet politics. The limiting case is Stewart (1969), a careful study of the repeal in 1964 of Khrushchev's scheme for "production education." Stewart argues that a lower elite-level political grouping, cutting across a number of Soviet institutions (themselves internally divided), coalesced on the specific issue of education, communicating its advocacy in advance of the involvement of Politburo-level leaders. Policy initiatives do not always "trickle down." Only later was the repeal issue seized upon by Khrushchev's

[68] Useful surveys of the recent "interest group" literature, in addition to Skilling and Griffiths' book, are Stewart (1969), Rigby (1970), Brown (1971, 1972), and Langsam and Paul (1972).

top-level political opponents as an instrument of factional struggle; this represented a nexus of interest group activity and elite conflict that, in the Soviet context, signified sharing of political power.

Stewart's conclusion rests on the resolution of two issues not definitely clarified in the study: whether a "vital" political issue was involved, and just when and how it became of interest to the Politburo. Nevertheless, Stewart's conceptualization, derived from Western interest group theory, is useful for its proposition that trans-institutional groupings coalesce in action on specific issues. Stewart carefully marshalls evidence from specialized Soviet media to support his case. This is an improvement over the frequently misleading imputation of uniform abstract "interests" to large bureaucratic organizations and professional and occupational groups, e.g., the "secret police," the "economic managers," the "Party apparatchiki," etc.

An example of the latter tendency is to be found in Aspaturian (1966), who argues plausibly that the scope for diverse internal influences on Soviet foreign policy, as well as domestic policy, broadened in the early 1960s. But he treats these influences in terms of assumed vested interests of "social and institutional groups" in the USSR polarized along international tension or relaxation lines. Traditional sectors of the armed forces, heavy industrial managers, and professional party apparatchiki and ideologues are presumed to benefit from perpetuation of international tension, and therefore to promote aggressive foreign policies. On the other hand, the state bureaucracy, light industrial managers, cultural, professional, and scientific groups, and the Soviet "consumers" are seen as benefitting from international détente, and hence supportive of conciliatory policies. This treatment is unsatisfactory; the "groupings" are not coordinate, their internal differentiation is not considered; the foreign policy "interests" ascribed to them are absolutized; even if the characterizations have some validity, they are not directly relevant to decision-making. For example, assuming part of the Soviet military is a "hardline" advocate in international relations, this does not signify *a priori* support for risky foreign policy initiatives, such as the 1961 Berlin crisis. Where you stand does not depend in any such literal way on where you sit.

The same tendency is evident in the work of Lodge (1969), who employs quantitative content analysis of presumptive specialized elite publications to analyze group attitudes. He concludes that groups perceive themselves as such and that they manifest a desire to participate in the political process. But he does not distinguish between professional-functional versus policy influence "group" attributes, nor does he examine group activity in the context of specific issues.

Skilling and Griffiths (1971) and Ploss (1967), in contrast, emphasize the amorphous and internally divided nature of institutional and professional groups in the USSR. The empirical problem is to define the predisposition of individuals and suborganizations toward specific policy issues that may arise; Judy [69] attempts to do this with respect to Soviet economists. Wolfe (1973) examines the attitudes of various elite groupings toward SALT. Another case study in this genre is Kolkowicz (1967), whose analysis of institutional relations between the Communist Party and the Soviet military establishment is refined by a breakdown of competing and partly overlapping subgroups and organizations within the military (factors based on common wartime experiences, service branches, etc.).

Another set of studies examines the role of "groupings" of various kinds in particular policy decisions but draws more conservative conclusions than did Stewart. For example, Schwartz and Keech (1968) analyzed the 1958 education reform in the USSR. In another careful case study, they, too, conclude that a trans-institu-

[69] In Skilling and Griffiths (1971).

tional grouping coalesced in action on the specific issue. They note, however, that the "debate over educational reform clearly emanated from the central and highest power structure," evidently a measure intended by Khrushchev to increase his personal political power. Later, they conclude, the educational debate assumed a momentum and even direction of its own. "The coopted public exploited their opportunity to substantially influence and alter the policy outcome." Ploss's study (1965) of Soviet agricultural policy under Khrushchev, a more vital political issue, is even less disposed to attribute influence on policymaking to pressure from broader sections of the Soviet elite. Other recent case studies[70] are in that same spirit.

The literature contains only scattered efforts to extend the "interest group" approach to the study of Soviet foreign policy. An ambitious but unsuccessful attempt is Paul (1971), who proposes an input-output framework of Soviet decision-making, including "information processing" linkages between the Politburo and broader sections of the Soviet elite. Paul suggests an ordering of the types of international situations in which particular domestic factors, including "group interests," may play an important role. Four sets of "core" domestic variables and one set of external variables are defined and illustrated. Paul argues that the critical variable is the ability of the Politburo to reach consensus concerning proper action on specific issues, the consensus serving as the link between all other core variables and policy. He formulates a series of propositions about the decisionmaking process, e.g., the greater the ability of the Politburo to reach consensus, the more quickly and resolutely will action be taken, and the firmer the policy will tend to be; deferment of decision will tend to make policy cautious, defensive, and non-interventionist unless and until external events force a crisis decision; decisions taken in a crisis situation brought on by deferment of decision will tend to be more impulsive, less cautious, and more interventionist; the less a clear and direct threat to the USSR, the greater the divergence of Politburo opinions and the more consideration will be given to domestic political factors. The derivation of these propositions from the underlying framework is unclear. Nor (as will be discussed) are the propositions adequately tested in a case study of the Soviet invasion of Czechoslovakia.

Dallin (1969) provides a loose framework for linking domestic political factors, e.g., resource allocation decisions, to Soviet foreign policy decisionmaking in the late Khrushchev period. These linkages include "interest groups" and broader public opinion; Dallin is concerned with explaining the departure of the Soviet case from the "ideal type" of linkages in a developing country. Recommending a "conflict model" of Soviet elite politics for analyzing foreign as well as domestic decisionmaking, Dallin notes cases where intra-leadership conflict on foreign policy was evident to outside observers at the time and other cases where the unity assumed to exist at the time was subsequently shown to have been a facade. Such leadership conflict, Dallin argues, has institutional referents. Moreover, individual leaders tend to adopt generally consistent positions on both domestic and foreign policy which can be grouped into two distinct clusters—"left" and "right." This framework may be useful as an organizing device, but the sharp differentiation between "left" and "right" policy clusters appears to be too rigid. Application of the framework is not demonstrated, and Dallin cautions that it is least applicable to Soviet crisis behavior.

Tatu (1969) affirms that "lobbies," often internally divided, affect Soviet foreign policy decisionmaking, and that the "pressure" of broader social forces is beginning to exert an influence on Soviet external behavior. But his analysis of specific Soviet foreign policy decisions between 1960 and 1966 pays little attention to the play of these forces. Rather, like Linden, Tatu traces a history of personal conflict between

[70] Collected in Juviler and Morton (1967), and Dallin and Westin (1966).

Khrushchev and his top-level opponents in the Kremlin over foreign as well as domestic policy issues.

Hutchings (1971) employs correlational analysis to explore the role of the Soviet military in Soviet foreign policy decisionmaking. He finds that Soviet defense spending generally declined before and increased after major international crises. His speculative conclusion is that Soviet military leaders have been instrumental in provoking crises in order to increase military budgets. This generalization, contradicting most interpretations of the history of party-military relations in the Soviet Union, is unsupported by any evidence demonstrating causality.

Organizational Process

Section II has described the "organizational process" approach to the study of decisionmaking and reviewed some of the works employing this approach that have examined foreign policy decisionmaking in Washington. To date this approach may correctly be termed "Americanology"; there exists only a handful of applications to other countries. There is in the literature no full-fledged attempt and few partial efforts to apply the approach to Soviet decisionmaking.

Allison (1971) applies the organizational process approach to Soviet behavior during the Cuban missile crisis. Allison uses this case study (treated separately later in this section) to generalize broadly, and contends that, "with a minimum of information about the organizations that constitute a government and their routines and SOP (standard operating procedures), an analyst can significantly improve some expectations generated by the Rational Actor Model" (p. 96). However, if the "minimum of information" amounts to no more than an understanding of the broad general characteristics of organizational behavior, employment of the organizational process approach tends toward a reductionist analysis which says, in effect, that a particular outcome occurred because the organizations involved in decisionmaking and implementation happen to "work that way." Moreover, poor information about particular decisionmaking organizations makes such analyses especially vulnerable to the effects of changes in organizational behavior. Finally, with a weak data base the range of behaviors compatible with the characteristics imputed to the organizations in question (from a "general understanding" of the way organizations function) may be very extensive. Even with good data, the outcomes of interactions of competing bureaucratic organizations are unlikely to be highly predictable.

A good illustration of the limits of the approach, in the absence of detailed evidence, is the significance Allison attaches in his study to the organizational strength of the Soviet Air Defense Forces (PVO). The organizational clout of the PVO is cited repeatedly to explain anomalies in Soviet military force posture (large deployments of anti-air defense weapons technically unsuited to the threat) and the seemingly contradictory Soviet behavior in the mid-1960s of pushing détente with the West and ABM deployment simultaneously. In the absence of information about the *actual* relationship between the PVO organization and the policy issues in question, the "organizational process" analyst would presumably have predicted that the Soviet government would reject a treaty with the United States banning more than token ABM deployments. In retrospect, he might "explain" the treaty as a defeat for PVO in bureaucratic infighting. With "minimum information," the analyst can say little more than this: If outcome X (favorable to institutional interests of organization (a) occurred, it was because (a) prevailed over (b), (c), and (d); if unfavorable outcome Y occurred, it was because (b), (c), and (d) prevailed over (a).

Triska and Finley (1968, Chapter 2) employ an information processing perspective in their examination of state and party institutions involved in Soviet foreign policy decisionmaking. They suggest that the bureaucratic processes of the respective institutions affect policy outcomes. Since they do not discuss the nature of such influence in general or with reference to specific cases, their discussion does not address the needs of the practicing analyst.

Glassman (1968) suggests that alternative foreign policy teams of varying numbers of "players" are involved in Soviet foreign policy decisionmaking from issue to issue. Involvement of a broader elite group results when initial consensus in Politburo subgroups is lacking. Projecting from his own review of Soviet decisionmaking in the early 1920s, as well as the works of Slusser (1967) and Ploss (1965), Glassman hypothesizes that the "players" manipulate information channels, with the Central Committee Secretariat foreign affairs machinery playing the key role. Hypotheses are explicitly labeled as such. Glassman makes no attempt to test or apply them and their derivation from the historical record he explicitly reviews is not obvious. The only evident utility of the work for the practitioner is the suggestion of a conceptual framework.

In the related area of Soviet defense decisionmaking, Marshall (1966, 1971) argues that unitary-rational explanations of Soviet weapons development are inadequate. The process can be better understood, he suggests, by employing an organizational perspective (by assuming, for example, that the proportional allocation of the Soviet defense budget among the respective Soviet military services remains relatively constant from year to year and that doctrinal disputes in the Soviet military press are related specifically to organizational concerns of individual military services). Alexander (1970, 1973) examines the weapons acquisition process in the Soviet Union, comparing it with the analogous process in France and the United States and emphasizing the impact of cultural-bureaucratic differences on organizational behavior in the three countries. Gallagher and Spielmann (1972) refer to several instances of Soviet weapons development which, they suggest, might be studied from an organizational perspective. These are all reasonable suggestions. But there is no example of an empirical study of a major Soviet foreign or defense policy decision employing an organizational process approach.[71] Nor has the effort been made to show how this approach might be operationalized to handle Soviet data and the Soviet decisionmaking environment.

SUPPLEMENTARY THEORIES

Cognitive Theory

As applied to the Soviet context, cognitive theory attempts to specify the "rationality" of Soviet leaders, asking how they "approach the task of making calculations, of deciding what objective to select, and how to deal with uncertainty and risk—that is, more generally, how to relate means and ends, etc."[72] The approach is often employed impressionistically, for example, by Ulam (1968), who emphasizes the largely idiosyncratic psychological factor in the relationship between Kennedy and Khrushchev. The seminal work in this genre is Leites (1953), who derives from the utterances of the founders of the Soviet Union an "operational code" mediating Bolshevik doctrine and Soviet behavior. Leites' distinctive psychoanalytically ori-

---

[71] On a lower-level non-military R&D issue, Campbell (1973) studies the debate in Soviet aviation circles on building a new airship, concluding that the outcome is to be understood primarily in terms of organizational competition; however, high level decisionmakers were apparently not closely involved.

[72] George (1969), p. 171.

ented approach, which relates the role of ideology to ego maintenance of Soviet leaders, has not been emulated by other scholars, but propositions from his "operational code" have influenced a whole generation of Soviet foreign affairs analysts.

Leites (1964) later appraised the validity of the Bolshevik "operational code" in the Khrushchev era. Much of the original code, he concludes, retained its force; the traditional Bolshevik fear of penetration by the enemy persisted, for example, as did willingness to retreat when absolutely necessary, but not before. On the other hand, the Bolshevik image of a "total adversary" had declined to some extent; Bolshevik leaders' fears of annihilation may have been mitigated.

Echoing a call of Bronfenbrenner (1964), and drawing centrally on Leites' work, George (1969) has urged renewed attention to the "neglected" operational code or "approach to political calculation."

> Knowledge of the actor's approach to calculating choice of action does not provide a simple key to explanation and prediction; but it can help the researcher and policy planner to "bound" the alternative ways in which the subject may perceive different types of situations and approach the task of making a rational assessment of alternative courses of action. Knowledge of the actor's beliefs helps the investigator to clarify the general criteria, requirements, and norms the subject attempts to meet in assessing opportunities that arise to make desirable gains, in estimating the costs and risks associated with them, and in making utility calculations.[73]

George puts forward a research construct for "operational codes" which distinguishes between "philosophical content"—e.g., the degree of harmony versus conflict in the political world; the prospects for the realization of one's aims—and "instrumental beliefs"—e.g., calculations of goals, risks, and timing. Kelly and Fleron (1970) have appealed, more ambitiously, for development of a methodology applicable to the Soviet leadership capable of distinguishing between group and individual belief systems.[74] These potentially fruitful recommendations for research have yet to be pursued systematically by Sovietologists.[75] Angell and Singer (in Angell, Dunham, and Singer (1964)) analyze Soviet elite attitudes toward international affairs between 1957 and 1960, comparing them to counterpart American attitudes. They draw suggestive conclusions about differences and similarities in attitudes among the two elites. For example, the Soviet elite views U.S. foreign policy as far more "haphazard" than *vice versa;* both elites are skeptical about the peace-keeping capabilities of international organizations. Conclusions of this order might be utilized in constructing an "operational code." However, Singer and Angell's analysis rests on the questionable assumption that the Soviet and American elites hold a comparable range of values and that the functional subgroups into which they divide are equivalent.

A substantial literature dealing with "waning of ideology" in the Soviet Union has appeared, consisting largely of piecemeal examinations of selected aspects of Soviet domestic and foreign policy. Zimmerman (1973) argues that "any attempt to predict Soviet foreign policy (. . . with the exception of [policy toward] Eastern Europe) for the 1970s from doctrinally derived goals is likely to prove a fruitless endeavor" (p. 194). This view is based in part on his (1969) systematic description of the revised, less dichotomous world-view espoused in the 1960s by Soviet academi-

---

[73] George (1969), pp. 172-73.

[74] Kelman (1970) has made a similar appeal with regard to the general field of foreign policy.

[75] Studies bearing on elaboration of an "operational code" for the Chinese leadership are noted in George (1969), note 5. Hirsch and Leites (1969) examine the congruity of the belief system of the Czechoslovak Communist reformers in 1968 with the original Bolshevik "operational code."

cians and institutes (and his related analysis of the emergence of a discipline of "international relations" in the USSR).[76]

The implication of Zimmerman's argument is that the Soviet leaders' approach to political calculation has become so diffuse and secularized that it differs little in *character* from that of Western political leaders. The utility of his systematic description of Soviet international relations literature for constructing a Soviet leadership "operational code" depends on the assumptions one makes about the relationship between that literature and the beliefs of Politburo-level leaders. Unfortunately this relationship has not been examined systematically; evidence bearing on the issue is scarce and of low quality.

More useful for understanding Soviet policy than analysis of ideology, Zimmerman argues, is analysis of the personal and career backgrounds of the Soviet elite. As Welsh[77] points out, most studies of Communist politics have been "elite studies" in that they have concentrated on the actions of a small group of political leaders. But in recent years scholars have attempted to broaden the focus of such analyses beyond their traditional "Kremlinological" concern with patron-client groupings engaged in power struggle. Some of the newer studies, which tend to marshall data more systematically than in the past, seek to identify situational contexts of individuals which may effect the decisionmaking process. That context includes both personal and institutional referents (which means that some of the studies mentioned might also fall into the "bureaucratic politics" category). An ambitious goal of this genre is to relate changes in the elite character and composition to other changes in the political system.

"Elite analysis" has received growing attention in the past five years.[78] No systematic attempt has yet been made, however, to relate findings of this research to foreign policy issues.[79]

Triska and Finley (1968, Chapters 2-4) make a preliminary effort to relate analysis of background characteristics and the belief-system of Soviet decisionmakers. They identify the Soviet foreign policy decisionmaking elite and analyze it in terms of such background characteristics as social origin, training, and nature of recruitment. They then formulate propositions about the role of ideology in the decisionmaking process, some of which relate to background characteristics of elite members and others to context. An example of the former is the proposition that older members of the elite employ doctrinal stereotypes more frequently than do younger ones. An example of a contextual proposition is that doctrine has a greater impact on long-range planning and expectations than on routine, short-range analysis and decisions.

The propositions are tested by quantitative content analysis of foreign policy remarks contained in speeches delivered at the Twenty-Second CPSU Congress. For each speaker, a "doctrinal stereotype quotient" is formulated, a fraction representing the number of doctrinally stereotyped words or phrases in proportion to the total number of words in the respective statements. *Inter alia*, the two propositions just cited are said to be confirmed by this technique. Other propositions are said to be disconfirmed, for example, the proposition that Soviet decisionmakers are influenced more by doctrine in crisis situations than in non-crisis periods.

This approach may be useful in distinguishing gross changes in the influence of doctrine over time and the differentiated influence of doctrine on various sub-

---

76 See also Sontag (1970).

77 In Beck, *et al.* (1973).

78 Examples of this work are collected in Beck, *et al.* (1973), Kanet (1971), and Farrell (1970).

79 As for example Edinger and Searing (1967) have done with respect to French and West German elites.

categories of individuals in the Soviet foreign policy elite. As applied by Triska and Finley, however, the generalizations may be distorted by absence of an attempt to distinguish among elements of the ideology, e.g., according to George's "philosophical" and "instrumental" components or Brzezinski's (1967) triad of philosophical assumptions, doctrinal elements, and action programs. Triska and Finley's work has two other failings, in terms of utility to the foreign policy analyst. It does not attempt to relate propositions to *particular* decisions. Nor does it attempt to weigh even crudely the impact of "doctrine" as compared to other specific influences on Soviet decisionmakers.

Theories of Personality

Personal motives have traditionally received considerable attention in historical and biographic accounts of Soviet leaders, especially Lenin and Stalin. The most prominent psychohistorian of Stalin is Tucker (1963, 1973), who treats Stalin as a pathological personality. Leites' works (1953, 1964), discussed earlier, embody an effort to examine with psychoanalytical techniques the behavior of an elite grouping and to describe a "political culture." Bauer (1956) is a related effort. For the post-Stalin period, personal motives have been neglected. There is no psychohistorical biography of either Khrushchev or Brezhnev.

CASE STUDIES OF SOVIET DECISIONMAKING

In contrast to the rich accumulation of U.S. foreign policy case studies, the Soviet foreign policy case study literature is small, fragmented, and generally underdeveloped. This applies not only to theory-oriented works that employ case studies as vehicles for generating or testing hypotheses about crisis or foreign policy decisionmaking, but also to traditional historical-narrative case studies designed primarily to advance knowledge about a particular international crisis or foreign policy decision.

As the primary external actor in most major U.S. crisis decisionmaking situations since World War II, the Soviet Union has figured prominently in most U.S. foreign policy decisionmaking case studies. However, Soviet behavior has been treated in such studies not as an object of inquiry *per se*, but as an input to U.S. decisionmaking, part of the external setting in which U.S. decisionmakers have operated. The object of empirical research has been American decisionmakers' *perceptions* of Soviet behavior, not that behavior itself. Rarely have any new insights about Soviet foreign policy behavior or the Soviet decisionmaking process emerged from such work; few students of American foreign policy have either been equipped or found it necessary for their purposes to engage in original research on Soviet behavior.[80]

The small case study component of the academic literature on Soviet foreign policy is disproportionate both to the size of the general literature and to the intrinsic importance of Soviet crisis behavior for the broad field of international relations. Its underdeveloped state cannot reasonably be attributed to the distinctive intellectual predispositions or range of methodological competences and preferences of the scholars who populate the field. The conventional or particularist case study approach would normally have had strong appeal for the traditionally trained and area-studies-oriented scholars around whom the field of Soviet studies developed in

[80] A partial exception is Allison (1971), treated below.

the United States, yet few case studies have been produced by them; theory-oriented case studies are even sparser. It is clear that data constraints—an order of magnitude more severe than those encountered by students of American foreign policy—have discouraged substantial growth of a Soviet case study literature, even of the conventional, particularist type.

None of the Soviet foreign policy case studies examined in this review is guided by an explicit decisionmaking theoretical framework;[81] few either generate or test general hypotheses about Soviet foreign policy. To the extent that conceptual models of decisionmaking underlie the case studies, they are implicit and must be inferred by the reader from the manner in which the analyst frames the problems he addresses and from the patterns of inference he employs.

All of the studies except Allison's appear implicitly to fall primarily within the category of the analytic paradigm, assuming some form of comprehensive rationality on the part of the decisionmaking unit. The analyst's awareness of constraints on comprehensive rationality in Soviet decisionmaking is evident in almost all cases, and is explicitly dealt with in work that focuses on factional struggle attendant to Soviet foreign policy crises, but none of the studies exhibits a capability to measure with any sophistication the effects of bureaucratic political constraints on the content of policy outputs. Apart from Paul (1971) and Slusser (1973), the unit of analysis in the cases reviewed is a unitary rational actor: the Soviet Union or the ranking party leader. Slusser, on the other hand, presents an extreme case of decisionmaking disaggregation, arguing that during the 1961 Berlin crisis, neither the head of the party and government, nor the collective party leadership, was capable of making binding decisions. Such factional struggle studies typically assume that one view or another prevails absolutely; opposition is either overcome or power changes hands.

While Sovietologists' choice of a unitary rational actor framework or of a "conflict model" which seems to generate *kto-kovo* (who defeats whom) scenarios rather than compromised decisions may in part reflect a particular conceptualization of decisionmaking in general or of the Soviet policy process in particular, the severely limited information at his disposal tends to drive the Sovietologist in any case toward utilization of such analytical frameworks. High level political decisionmaking in the Soviet Union, as elsewhere, generates observable outputs, but the policy process itself, particularly with respect to sensitive foreign and military policy issues, is carefully concealed. Hence, the dominant pattern of inference moves backward from "action" (observable policy outputs) to "intention" (policy inputs), on the working assumption that the process by which the latter is transformed into the former is guided by some form of comprehensive or limited rationality the logic of which the analyst can attempt to reproduce. The Soviet decisionmaking process is "black-boxed," even if the scholar believes that it covers a complex, differentiated structure of organizations and individuals pursuing goals that are competing and inconsistent, because access to that structure and information about its operations is simply not available to him.

Scholars of Soviet foreign policy lack a sufficiently detailed or authoritative data base from which to write the most elementary, strictly journalistic account of Soviet behavior in any post-war crisis comparable in verifiable accuracy to, say, what a team of *New York Times* investigative reports are ordinarily able to piece together within weeks of a major U.S. foreign policy decision. The Sovietologist making a comparable effort would soon find himself absorbed in generating surrogates for

---

[81] This applies to the case studies written by Sovietologists; the Allison study (1971) employs the Cuban missile crisis, including Soviet policy issues, as a vehicle for demonstrating the explanatory power of three alternative decisionmaking models.

data that are considered starting points by his colleagues examining crisis behavior of the U.S. Government. Key elements in a basic narrative account must usually be reconstructed from inferences that are several times removed from "hard" evidence, and the analysis must be built on a pyramid of such inferences, virtually precluding findings that can be presented with high confidence.[82] What is produced, often ingeniously, by such efforts, is seldom persuasive enough to gain wide acceptance in the field, so that the storehouse of established knowledge from which new studies may draw grows very slowly and unevenly.

Indeed, to speak at all about a Soviet foreign policy case study literature, much less a literature on crisis decisionmaking, is to stretch a point: There is not a single study on the Soviet Union that remotely approximates, in quality or comprehensiveness, the exemplary Western case studies identified in Sec. II. Indeed, it would be more correct to speak of "case illustrations" than of "case studies" in describing the bulk of the literature dealing with Soviet foreign policy. The major post-war international crises (Iran, Turkey, Berlin, Cuba, the Middle East, etc.) figure prominently in all of the general studies of Soviet foreign policy, but typically the treatment is episodic and illustrative, rather than comprehensive or systematic,[83] or else, less frequently, schematic crisis material is highly aggregated for special purposes, as in the Triska/Finley (1968) analysis of Soviet risk-taking propensities.

The "major" Soviet foreign policy case studies in the literature are identified in the following pages. For the most part, the authors of these monographs intended to provide comprehensive or partial explanation of Soviet behavior in a particular crisis, consistent with the limited data at their disposal. Brief "case illustrations" in general works on Soviet foreign policy have been excluded, with the exception of a few of the more ambitious efforts (e.g., measured in length—more than ten pages). One or two studies attempting partial explanations of some particular aspect of Soviet crisis behavior have also been included for special purposes. The case studies surveyed have been grouped by reference to particular crises. While the listing is not exhaustive, the limited number of crises mentioned is not an accident of the selection. There are no case studies of Soviet policy or behavior extant in the academic literature for many of the most important post-war international crises in which the Soviet Union has been a major actor. For example, the outbreak of the Korean War, probably the second most popular source of crisis studies in the U.S. foreign policy literature after the Cuban missile crisis, has not inspired a single case study by a Soviet specialist.

Berlin (1948, 1958-59, 1961-62)

There is an extensive case study literature by non-Soviet specialists on the intermittent Berlin crises since 1948,[84] and Berlin crises are treated in varying detail in most general accounts of U.S. foreign policy during the post-war period. But there are few monographs written from the perspective of Soviet decisionmaking. Speier's is the only work by a non-Soviet specialist that attempts an independent analysis of Soviet behavior (in the 1958-59 crisis), but for the specialized purpose of constructing an anatomy of Soviet political blackmail. Among works by Soviet affairs specialists, the Horelick/Rush study (1966) of the relationship between strategic power and Soviet foreign policy devotes one chapter to the USSR's Berlin

---

[82] See, for example, Mackintosh's (1973) speculative reconstruction of the role which the Soviet military leadership may have played in three cases of foreign policy decisionmaking.

[83] See Mackintosh (1962), Ulam (1968, 1971), and Tatu (1969).

[84] Davison (1958), Speier (1961), Smith (1963), and Schick (1971).

policy in the late 1950s and early 1960s; but, as in the Speier study, Horelick and Rush examine it as a specialized case of the political use of Soviet strategic power during the Khrushchev era. There is episodic and case-illustrative treatment of Berlin in most of the general work on post-war Soviet foreign policy.[85]

Slusser's (1973) work on the 1961 Berlin crisis is unique in the Soviet foreign policy literature in that it is the only book-length study that purports to be devoted to analysis of a single case. But this is less a function of its comprehensiveness with respect to Soviet decisionmaking in the 1961 crisis than of the author's methodology, which entails a detailed chronological account of all of the major policy issues, domestic as well as international, confronting the Soviet leadership from the onset of the crisis in June 1961 to its termination after the Twenty-Second Party Congress in October 1961. Thus, some 40 percent of the text is devoted to a detailed analysis of the composition of delegates to the Congress and their speeches on a broad range of subjects, substantively remote from the Berlin crisis, which are inferentially related to Berlin as evidence of factional struggle in which Berlin policy is said to have been a central issue.

Slusser's study is not informed by any particular theory of decisionmaking; nor does it generate broad hypotheses about Soviet foreign policy decisionmaking behavior. It does address the problem of Soviet policy formation during a particular historical span, namely the period before the ouster of Nikita Khrushchev in 1964. In the Soviet context, it may be regarded as falling within the category of studies that approach decisionmaking from a "Kremlinological" (or bureaucratic politics) perspective. It is perhaps the most radical case study of that genre, concluding with the finding of "a power struggle more intense, more violent, and more divisive than had previously been suspected, a situation in which power lay at times in the hands of a single leader, at times was shared by a collective leadership, and at times seemed to be up for grabs, with whoever could grasp the levers of power entitled to operate them" (p. ix).

The technique employed is familiar: content analysis of the official Soviet documents, leaders' speeches, and other press materials. What is novel in Slusser's study is its reliance on inferences derived from data on the physical location of Soviet leaders at times when major new policy pronouncements of the Soviet Government were published in the central press (a case of "locusology" supplementing "Kremlinology"). Khrushchev's absence from or presence in Moscow on the occasion of the publication of major Soviet policy pronouncements appears to be the crucial variable in inferring whether a given Soviet crisis "move" was initiated by him or by his presumed factional opponents. The persuasiveness of the argument rests largely on the extent to which the reader is prepared to infer causality from such correlations and is reduced by Slusser's failure to deal with "intervening variables" (such as the use of the telephone and telegraph by political leaders) and communication strategies for timing publication of declaratory policy documents.

Middle East Crises (Suez and the Six-Day War), 1956 and 1967

The Suez crisis of 1956 has been the subject of numerous case studies, but most intensively from the perspective of Anglo-French and American relations.[86] Among studies of Soviet foreign policy, Laqueur's (1959) volume on Soviet Middle Eastern policy includes a short chapter on the Soviet role in the 1956 crisis, but not a

[85] Ulam (1968, 1971), Mackintosh (1962), Tatu (1969), Dinerstein (1968), and Wolfe (1970).
[86] Thomas (1966), and Neustadt (1970).

comprehensive case study. The only more or less systematic narrative account found in the literature is Smolansky (1965), which explicitly addresses the major questions of Soviet policy raised by the crisis. A straightforward historical account, Smolansky's case study treats the Soviet Government as a unitary decisionmaker and builds the analysis almost exclusively on an examination of published Soviet decision outputs: diplomatic notes and letters and accompanying Soviet press commentary. By contrast, Ra'anan (1969), in a study of the 1955 Soviet proxy arms deal with Egypt which helped set the stage for the 1956 Suez crisis, places heavy emphasis on factional struggle within the Soviet leadership during this period. As in other Soviet foreign policy case studies oriented on the "Kremlinological" approach, evidence of factional struggle is drawn almost exclusively from content analysis of the public utterances of Soviet leaders, or of their presumed surrogates writing for publication. Ra'anan concludes that the new Soviet Middle East policy of the mid-1950s encountered strong resistance from an important leadership faction, which was overcome by Khrushchev, but the study does not show how the substance of policy outputs was affected by factional dispute.

Although Soviet involvement in the Middle East crisis of June 1967 was weightier and more prominent than in the Suez crisis, there are still no detailed Soviet case studies. Among the broad studies of the crisis, Laqueur's (1968) provides the fullest treatment of the Soviet role, but it emphasizes the impact of Soviet behavior on the policies and actions of the belligerents rather than the Soviet decisionmaking process *per se*.[87] Horelick[88] compares selected characteristics of Soviet crisis behavior in the 1956 and 1967 Middle East crises, but provides a detailed case study of neither.

Quemoy Crisis, 1958

Of the several case studies of the 1958 Quemoy crisis, only one, Thomas (1962), analyzes that event from the Soviet perspective. The Thomas study is a comprehensive account of the major Soviet moves during the crisis, but it is focused on strains in the Sino-Soviet alliance occasioned by the crisis. Thomas treats the Soviet Union throughout as a unitary actor. Suggestions of vacillation and shifts in policy are not attributed to multilateral decisionmaking. The principal finding of the study is that the Soviet Government exhibited reluctance to support the PRC in a test of U.S. intentions that involved the risk of military conflict.[89]

The Cuban Missile Crisis, 1962

This is easily the most extensively analyzed and, on the U.S. side, the most richly documented U.S.-Soviet crisis. But, with few exceptions, the focus of these studies is on U.S. decisionmaking. Of the U.S. decision-oriented studies, only Allison's (1971) treats the Soviet side systematically. Two of the three questions examined from the perspective of Allison's alternative decisionmaking models concern Soviet decisions: Why were the missiles emplaced in Cuba, and why were they withdrawn? But the most comprehensive analysis is reserved for the third question: Why did the United States choose the blockade option? Allison's most detailed

---

[87] Nor do the accounts in Ulam (1968, 1971) and Tatu (1969) devote much attention to the Soviet policy process.

[88] In Becker and Horelick (1970).

[89] This finding is contradicted by Halperin and Tsou (in Halperin (1967)), who also analyze the 1958 Quemoy crisis primarily from the perspective of Sino-Soviet relations and conclude that "there may not have been any major Sino-Soviet disagreement about strategy during the crisis."

analysis of Soviet decisionmaking is contained in his Model I (unitary rational actor) cut at the problem, and here his explicit approach parallels the one implicitly employed by most Soviet specialists in their case studies. Allison's Model II (organizational process) analysis deals at some length with the emplacement and withdrawal of the Soviet missiles, but concentrates on policy *implementation* by Soviet organizations in the field rather than on high level decisionmaking.[90] For lack of available relevant evidence, Allison's Model III (bureaucratic politics) analysis says little about Soviet decisionmaking, focusing rather on the U.S. decision to impose the blockade. There is no synthesis or integrated model, and the three parallel case studies included in the work are uneven with respect to scope, coverage, and the Soviet decisionmaking issues examined.

Of the broad studies of Soviet foreign policy by Soviet affairs specialists, Ulam (1968, 1971) and Tatu (1969) contain narrative accounts of the Cuban missile crisis from the perspective of Soviet decisionmakers; Horelick (1964) is the standard monograph in the Soviet field. All these works treat Soviet decisionmaking in the Cuban crisis from a unitary actor perspective, explicitly identifying Khrushchev as the prime mover on the Soviet side. Ulam interprets Soviet objectives in terms of an elaborate scenario according to which Khrushchev, had he not been compelled to withdraw the missiles, would have appeared at the United Nations in November 1962 and proposed a dramatic omnibus package, offering to withdraw the missiles in return for a German peace treaty, including an absolute prohibition of nuclear weapons for the FRG, and a nuclear-free zone in the Pacific, including a pledge by the PRC not to acquire nuclear weapons. Tatu stresses Berlin as the focal point of Soviet objectives in deploying missiles in Cuba, while Horelick interprets the Soviet move as designed to redress the unfavorable U.S.-Soviet strategic nuclear balance, and, hence to strengthen the USSR's position on a whole range of international issues, particularly Berlin.

Czechoslovakia (1968)

Although there is a large literature on the Soviet invasion of Czechoslovakia,[91] there are few case studies that examine Soviet decisionmaking in any detail. The Czechoslovak side is heavily documented, and the most detailed material purporting to describe Soviet behavior in crisis negotiations with the Czechoslovak leaders comes from Czechoslovak sources.[92]

Ermarth (1969) provides the most comprehensive effort to reconstruct the calculations leading to the Soviet decision to invade, laying out and examining four alternative hypotheses: (1) duplicity by Dubcek at Cierna, the official Soviet justification; (2) duplicity by the Soviet leaders (Cierna and Bratislava as holding actions while the invasion was organized); (3) a breakdown of the Soviet collective leader-

---

[90] Moreover, the major conclusion does not flow directly from assumptions about organizational behavior, but from a conjecture about a deliberately self-serving reinterpretation of Politburo orders by the Strategic Rocket Forces that strains credibility. Allison suggests that the Strategic Rocket Forces Command, instructed by the Politburo to "place missiles in Cuba," an order which Allison speculates was intended to mean MRBMs only, installed more provocative and expensive IRBMs as well, in order to secure better coverage of U.S. strategic targets, without informing the political leadership of such adjustments in "details." The only evidence offered in support of this conjecture is that Khrushchev, reporting after the event to the Supreme Soviet, stated that agreement was reached between the Soviet and Cuban Governments in the summer of 1962 to station a few dozen "*medium-range* ballistic missiles" in Cuba (p. 113). Unfortunately for this interpretation, public Soviet terminology does not distinguish between "medium-range" and "intermediate-range" missiles, but uses the term "*srednii*" (medium) to cover all strategic missiles with less than intercontinental range.

[91] Lowenthal (1968), Ermarth (1969), James (1969), Windsor and Roberts (1969), Hodnett and Potichnyj (1970), Paul (1971), Remington (1971), and Tigrid (1971).

[92] See especially Tigrid (1971).

ship; (4) a post-Bratislava change in Politburo perceptions and a new consensus culminating in the reluctant order to use military force. Ermarth finds the fourth explanation, modified by elements of the first three hypotheses, most persuasive. The methodology is "selective historical narrative."

Hodnett and Potichnyj (1970) is a detailed and systematic examination of the involvement of the Ukrainian factor in the Soviet-Czechoslovak crisis and of its bearing on the Soviet decision to invade. It does not attempt to estimate the weight of the factor in the making of that decision, nor to offer a comprehensive explanation of it. It is described by its authors as a case study of participation by one Soviet republic in relations between the Soviet Union and Eastern Europe. Rosenau's (1969) linkage framework for examining the relationship between domestic and external determinants of foreign policy is adapted as an organizing device. Within the explicitly limited confines of what the authors set out to do, the study makes a persuasive case that Ukrainian leaders were consulted in earnest about Soviet policy toward Czechoslovakia and that considerations of particular relevance to the Ukraine contributed to the ultimate Politburo decision to invade.

Paul (1971) also relates external and internal determinants of the Soviet decision to invade Czechoslovakia in terms of the linkage theory adapted from Rosenau, but, as already described, attempts to provide a comprehensive rather than a partial explanation of that decision. The methodology is operationalized through content analysis of Soviet press coverage of Czechoslovak developments during three selected periods in 1968. *Pravda, Izvestiia, Red Star,* and *Trud* are presumed to reflect the views of the Communist Party, the government bureaucracy, the military establishment, and the Central Council of Trade Unions, respectively, and, by extrapolation, Politburo members and other Soviet leaders at the head of these organizations. Perceptual differences among the leaders are inferred from divergencies in the number of articles coded favorable, hostile, and neutral toward the Dubcek regime in the respective newspapers during the selected periods, and inferences about the course of consensus formation in the Politburo are drawn from these correlations. Findings are asserted to confirm the propositions described earlier in this section about the relationship between the Politburo's ability to reach consensus and the nature of Soviet policy. While the propositions are plausible, the evidence adduced to confirm them is questionable. Individual Politburo leaders are identified by flat assumption with views inferred from press materials on Czechoslovakia coded according to judgments of implicit attitude that are displayed only summarily. (It is suggested on the strength of ambivalence about Czechoslovakia displayed in *Izvestiia's* columns, that both President Podgorny and Premier Kosygin may have opposed the invasion, since both "represented" the government in the Politburo). The number of references in the respective newspapers from which leader attitudes during the time periods selected are drawn is very small (from five to twenty per month for the major press organs) and the computations do not distinguish among types of materials, e.g., TASS dispatches versus commentaries. Finally, given the small numbers in the sample, the variance between *Izvestiia* and other press organs (e.g., *Red Star)* does not seem large enough to support the conclusions drawn from it. The study demonstrates many of the difficulties involved in the employment of Soviet press materials to disaggregate the top Soviet decisionmaking units.

RECAPITULATION

Conclusions from the review of Sovietology in this section are the following:
1. *Sovietologists have attempted since the mid-1960s to integrate Soviet studies*

into the social science mainstream, but with little attention to a decision-theory perspective. Comparative Communist studies have been the major focus of this effort. Systematic investigation of relationships between inputs and outputs have treated the decision process as a "black box" in the aggregated analytic paradigm. The resulting partial theories have been pitched at such a level of generality that, questions of validation aside, their utility to the practicing foreign policy analyst is narrowly limited. Taxonomies in this literature may suggest new elements of an issue to the foreign policy analyst; in the absence of a theory relating the various inputs and outputs, much of the work will seem like mere proceduralism. Some of this work is notable for its spirit of innovation and experimentation, but much of it fails to meet high standards with respect to sound research design, explicit use of reasoned assumptions, and careful treatment of data.

2. *Foreign policy studies of the Soviet Union have been little affected by the new strivings in Sovietology.* Broad propositions about Soviet foreign policy behavior have been advanced intermittently but not systematically; there has been little cumulation of comparable hypotheses and propositions. Techniques of modern social science have been introduced, but on an ad hoc basis with little regard to a theoretical or conceptual framework.

3. *Promising studies on policy-relevant "Kremlinology" and studies with a broader "interest grouping" focus have been produced, but primarily with regard to Soviet domestic politics.* A broadened "Kremlinological" literature has devoted more attention to policy as opposed simply to power struggle among Soviet leaders. An exploratory "interest grouping" literature examines the broader constituencies and other wellsprings of the behavior of top leaders as they coalesce in action on specific policy issues; this is an improvement over imputing uniform and abstract interests to large bureaucratic organizations and social groups. But the literature exhibits only fragmentary application to foreign policy issues.

4. *The "organizational process" context of Soviet foreign policy decisions has largely been neglected;* the approach suggests pertinent questions which are, however, difficult to answer in the Soviet data context. Efforts to apply the approach in the absence of a minimum of Soviet data carry the danger of reductionist analysis.

5. *Potentially fruitful suggestions for studies to illuminate the belief system of Soviet decisionmakers have not been followed up.* The "operational code" approach to the cognitive universe of top leaders has been neglected; piecemeal components have been distinguished, but these are uneven and attempts at synthesis are lacking. Greater effort has been devoted (under the rubric "elite analysis") to the situational contexts of key decisionmakers—again, emphasizing domestic policy issues. Major psychohistorical analyses of post-Stalinist Soviet leaders do not exist.

6. *The case study literature on Soviet crisis behavior is too underdeveloped to provide an adequate data base for purposes of theory-building or other generalization.* Only "case illustrations" exist, not major case studies.

IV. CONCLUSIONS

This report has reviewed the general social science theoretical literature on decisionmaking and, from a decision-related perspective, recent analytical literature on the conduct of Soviet foreign policy. We concluded that *no model derived from available theory can be expected to provide comprehensive and consistent explanations and reliable and accurate predictions with respect to the kinds of foreign policy and crisis decisions of interest to the Soviet policy analyst.* Whatever merit there may be to the argument that the quality of Soviet foreign policy analysis has been retarded by the failure of policy analysts to attend systematically to developments in decision theory and to models derived from it, that failure does not include inadvertent neglect of a full-fledged, on-the-shelf "model" of foreign policy decision-making capable of revolutionizing the analytical state of the art.

Whether such an empirical model of decisionmaking can eventually be derived from decision theory must remain an open question, in essence, philosophical.[93] Meanwhile the analyst of Soviet foreign policy must address the questions at hand and provide the best answers he can within the theoretical state of the art and the limits of the imperfect data base available to him. *The decisionmaking literature—including the underdeveloped cybernetic paradigm—suggests multiple perspectives on the phenomena under examination which might improve the analyst's work.*

We have pointed out in Sec. II some advantages and limitations of the applications of decisionmaking theory that affect its utility for foreign policy analysis. With respect to the study of Soviet foreign policy decisionmaking, the limitations are compounded by severe data constraints, which are generally acknowledged. Furthermore, the questionable "fit" of the Soviet Union into the broader theoretical framework based on Western—and specifically, the American—decisionmaking process is still a controversial and unresolved issue.

The body of Sovietological literature, discussed in Sec. III, reflects a considerable effort to integrate contemporary social science methodologies and techniques into fields of inquiry that have until recently remained aloof from them. *But the impact of social science decisionmaking theory and of empirical work in the non-Soviet field employing decision-oriented theoretical approaches has been marginal. The utility of this literature as it now stands for the practicing analyst of Soviet foreign policy is limited.* The search for "theory" based on systematic investigation of relationships among policy "inputs" and "outputs" has been relatively overemphasized; the decision-theory perspective has greater potential utility for the analyst who seeks to provide explanations and predictions of the behavior of foreign governments to U.S. policymakers.

It is still difficult to reconcile major differences in perspective between the theory-building enterprise, on one hand, and the practical objectives of the policy analyst, on the other. The *goal* of the theorist is in harmony with the needs of the practicing analyst: to develop theoretical generalizations which specify conditions under which given types of behavior can be expected. But the process of developing theory creates a difference in perspective, for the theorist must of necessity first emphasize plausible generalizations and then turn to the task of refinement and qualification. The theorist strives first for rigor, parsimony, and the formulation of propositions at a level of generality high enough to apply to the largest possible set

[93] See Gorman (1970).

of observable phenomena. The foreign policy analyst, on the other hand, is apt to be concerned above all with variables critically relevant to his particular problem that are not covered by the generalizations derived from the theorist's model. As George, *et al.* (1971), point out, the foreign policy analyst is preoccupied with "policy relevant variation among particular cases" rather than with broad-spanning generalizations. The scholar will prefer a simpler, less encompassing theory that can establish linkage between the variables with high confidence. The foreign policy analyst needs what George terms a "rich" theory that tries to encompass many policy-relevant variables (including "soft" and "spongy" ones), even though such a theory may not be susceptible to rigorous verification.

No matter how "rich" such a theory may be, it will still be incomplete when applied to a single case; and the analyst will be obliged to combine judgment and intuition with generalizations derived from theory in order to fill gaps. The quality of that judgment and intuition will depend heavily on the analyst's detailed, though imperfect, knowledge of the case at hand. Successful manipulation of even the most rigorous scientific model must be based on a solid foundation of prior established knowledge. With respect to the study of Soviet foreign policy, both the theoretical constructs available and the foundation of prior established knowledge are deficient.

First priority should therefore go to (a) improving and enlarging the established knowledge base about the context of Soviet foreign policy decisionmaking in ways that render that knowledge susceptible to disciplined inquiry and (b) to formulating and testing decisionmaking theories in the middle range that are specific to what is known and can be learned about the Soviet decisionmaking context. These two undertakings are closely related. As indicated in Sec. II, analytic and cybernetic decisionmaking paradigms and the theories they generate can broaden the foreign policy analyst's perspective and provide him with a coherent logical structure for disciplining his inquiry. They can also organize and inform his search for new knowledge better able to meet the distinctive data demands of decision-theory-oriented approaches. Hopefully, significant improvement in the data base will, in turn, facilitate the formulation of a richer set of hypotheses about Soviet decisionmaking and, eventually, the development of decisionmaking theories more susceptible to application and testing in the Soviet context than those presently available.

The results achieved in the better recent case studies of U.S. foreign policy decisionmaking that have focused on organizational process and bureaucratic politics variables suggest the desirability of a shift in Soviet foreign policy studies toward more systematic attention to internal determinants of policy and toward disaggregation of the decisionmaking units involved. Far more is known about the external setting of Soviet foreign policy decisionmaking (the state of the world, external regional military-political environments, military capabilities and dispositions of opponents, etc.) than about its internal environment. It is largely for this reason, apart from the conceptual lenses worn by foreign policy analysts, that most efforts to provide comprehensive explanations or systematic contingent predictions of Soviet external behavior have focused on the interaction between the Soviet decisionmaking unit, treated essentially as a unitary rational actor constrained by factors and forces that are poorly understood, and the external environment, which can usually be described in comparatively rich detail.

In this connection, efforts in the theoretical literature to develop organizational process and bureaucratic politics approaches to foreign policy decisionmaking are highly pertinent. While it is quite uncertain that the large number of relevant variables, diverse in nature and presenting data demands of great severity, can be structured and synthesized into a comprehensive and coherent analytical framework or model, the partial models or paradigms that have been elaborated may indicate to the foreign policy analyst pertinent data to look for and suggest interrelationships to explore. When the data are there or can be acquired or developed, the discipline and structure provided even by admittedly partial models seem capable of generating significant improvements in the work of the analyst of Soviet foreign policy. The following pages contain specific recommendations for improvements toward this end.

"Kremlinology"/Bureaucratic Politics

Paradoxically, the bureaucratic politics context which, both conceptually and with respect to its data demands, is regarded as more difficult to apply in the American decisionmaking context than competing conceptual frameworks, may have better prospects for fuller operationalization as an approach to the study of Soviet foreign policy decisionmaking. This is because of the substantial prior efforts of Soviet foreign policy students in "Kremlinological" analysis, to which the bureaucratic politics approach is closely related. As Allison (1971) notes, the evidential sources for such analysis must be participants in the decisionmaking process themselves. Failing direct access to participants, or supplementing it, bureaucratic politics analysis requires access to documents bearing on the intra-governmental bargaining process: diaries, discussions with close observers of the participants, or equivalent indirect evidence.

Analyses of Soviet foreign policy are, of course, many times further removed from such evidence than are their American-oriented counterparts. But the very remoteness of such sources has compelled Soviet analysts over the years to develop techniques for discovering and employing surrogates for such missing evidence. A primary technique is the deciphering of "esoteric communications" in public media concerning issues disputed among Soviet leaders. The quality of such surrogate evidence is necessarily inferior even to incomplete and fragmentary evidence of a more direct kind, such as is ordinarily available for analysts of U.S. decisionmaking. Uncertainty about the quality of that evidence is, except in rare circumstances, irreducible, since even good predictions about outcomes inferred from such evidence fail to provide high confidence validation that policy inputs supplied by "Kremlinological" analysis are correct. Nevertheless, given this background, application of a bureaucratic politics approach to the Soviet context does not raise the same risk of unjustifiable extrapolation from American experience as does the organizational process approach at its present stage of development.

The updated and broadened Kremlinology that is more sensitive to leadership policy conflicts, as described in Sec. III, has considerable potential and should receive more attention in foreign policy studies. It should be possible to refine further the "conflict model" of Soviet leadership behavior. One promising vehicle is comparative work across the different periods of the Soviet experience from Lenin to Brezhnev. Another is comparative work on such a "conflict model" across a number of different Leninist parties.

Within this framework, patron-client relationships deserve more attention. Comparatively little research has been done for the post-Khrushchev period on the study of the personal followings of top leaders—the Kremlinological concept of *shefstvo* (patronage). The relevant questions have been posed repeatedly.[94] What does the client offer the patron? Does the relationship entail joint involvement in irregular informal practices upon which the day-to-day functioning of the system depends?

---

[94] See Rigby, in "Kremlinology" (1964). The durability and importance of personal associations was recently reaffirmed by Andrei Sakharov (interview in *Dagens Nyheter*, Stockholm, July 3, 1973).

What explains the tenacity and longevity of such associations in Soviet politics? How many hierarchical levels do they embrace? How do career bonds compare with other common background characteristics in the formation of patron-client relationships? Reshetar (1955) suggested studying the promotions and demotions of several hundred secondary and tertiary officials as an indicator of jockeying for position at the top level. This has never been attempted systematically.[95] Such studies of patronage should not ignore rumor information as a source of surrogate data for generating hypotheses.

Studies of factions and patron-client relationships should be complemented by research with an "interest group" orientation intended to uncover broader referents of top-level decisionmaking. The evidential base is more pertinent to domestic decisionmaking in the Soviet Union, but it is relevant to foreign policy decisionmaking as well. Of the approaches reviewed in Sec. III, the "issue oriented" studies of "interests" as they coalesce in action on specific policy issues appear to be the most promising; additional case studies both large and small, along the lines of Stewart (1969) and Schwartz and Keech (1968), would be highly desirable. This is a more fruitful line of inquiry than attempting to characterize "attitudes" of large formal "groups" in an issue-free context.●Again, the relevant questions have often been posed. What is the common interest or other property defining the group? What are the salient contradictions with interests or characteristics of other groups? What is the mechanism for forming and articulating group opinion on current issues? What is the nature of the bond between the group and top political leaders? What is the access of a group to high level decisionmakers? What are the internal and external rules of behavior applicable to the pursuit of group goals? What degree of mobilization can be obtained by a particular group?[96]

Explicit foreign policy ramifications of "interest grouping" studies deserve more attention. Paul's (1971) typology of international situations in which broad domestic influences may play varying roles in decisionmaking warrants further development. Investigation of Dallin's (1969) suggestion that leaders' or groupings' positions on various domestic and foreign policies may fall into a comparatively small number of "clusters" might be fruitful.

Organizational Process

Of all the decision-theory-related analytical frames of reference surveyed in this report, the organizational process approach has thus far made the smallest impact on Soviet foreign policymaking studies. *Refining and operationalizing the organizational process approach to make a better "fit" with the Soviet decisionmaking environment deserves high priority.* Some critics of an organizational process approach to American foreign policy decisionmaking have argued that it underplays the power and independence of the President and thus overrates the influence of the bureaucracy.[97] Others have observed that it fails to allow for the effect of changes in organizational behavior, particularly in crisis conditions; indeed, a major premise of the approach is that organizational behavior changes little if at all. The force of these criticisms in the Soviet context needs to be carefully explored. For example, the Politburo's capacity to involve itself closely in decisionmaking at far lower levels

---

[95] A new design for such a study, which would manipulate a large volume of conflicting information of mixed reliability about such patron-client relationships, has been proposed by William R. Harris of The Rand Corporation.

[96] See Gehlen (1965), and Rigby, in "Kremlinology" (1964).

[97] E.g., Krasner (1972).

than is customary with regard to the Executive Branch in the United States is well established. It does not seem justified to assume fundamentally congruent influences of organizational and bureaucratic processes on Soviet and American decisionmaking.

Indeed, the utility of the organizational process approach applied against the *presently* available data base concerning Soviet organizations involved in the decisionmaking process is uncertain, as argued earlier with specific reference to Allison (1971). Allison acknowledges that in order for the [Model II] paradigm to get a strong grip on a specific case, it "must be fleshed out by information about the characteristics of the organizations involved." The information available to the scholar of Soviet foreign policy about the key organizations involved in the policy process is at best fragmentary, more often, nonexistent. In the realm of military policymaking, for example, even a simple table of organization can be assembled only with the aid of conjecture; the existence of key coordinating bodies must be inferred by reference to the logic of bureaucratic organizations; little is known about how these organizations operate in practice and even less about how they interact. [98]

In short, given the paucity of information available to scholars about Soviet organizations involved in foreign and military policy decisionmaking, there is no reason to believe that explanations or predictions of Soviet behavior deduced from assumptions about "organizational behavior in general" will be intrinsically more reliable than or even add much to those derived from unitary rational actor assumptions that essentially "black-box" the policy process.

The most immediate requirement for improving the utility of the organizational process approach for the analysis of Soviet foreign policy behavior is an intensified effort to explore Soviet organizational behavior in its own terms. Extrapolation from "general understanding" or from U.S. organizational behavior can inform that exploration, but can be used as substitutes for data on Soviet behavior only at high risk. Hard data bearing directly on the structure, composition, functions, and interactions of contemporary Soviet organizations participating in foreign policy decisionmaking are a high priority target, but will continue to be elusive.

Historical materials may help to overcome this gap. Comparatively little effort has been made to extract systematically from historical Soviet documents information pertaining to foreign policymaking organizations and process. There is now a substantial Soviet documentary and memoir literature covering the pre-war and World War II years; [99] the post-war period is only sparsely covered with low quality materials. While the internal setting of Soviet decisionmaking has changed greatly over the years, insights derived from a systematic examination of Soviet organizational behavior even in the distant past should be at least as relevant as what can be assumed about current Soviet organizational behavior from knowledge of foreign analogues; at the least, such insights may help to refine those assumptions and adapt them to the Soviet context.[100] Moreover, examination of historical materials from an organizational process perspective may in some instances provide suggestions for new case studies or for improvement of old ones written without the benefit of such organizational data.

Finally, information on present-day Soviet organizations not directly involved in foreign policy or military decisionmaking may provide valuable insights into

---

[98] For the best available treatment of Soviet military decisionmaking organizations, see Gallagher and Spielman (1972).

[99] Some of this literature is utilized, but for biographic purposes, in Chaney (1971).

[100] Glassman (1968) has made such a preliminary effort in his study of the Soviet Foreign Ministry in the 1920s. Fainsod (1958) offers insights into Soviet organizational behavior, but the captured Smolensk archive has not been exploited systematically for this purpose.

patterns of Soviet organizational behavior that could help fill some of the large gaps in knowledge about the more sensitive organizations.[101]

Cognitive Theory

Analysis of the belief systems of the Soviet political elite appears to have potential for enriching the study of Soviet decisionmaking, but remains underdeveloped. George's (1969) proposed research construct for developing an "operational code" to illuminate an actor's approach to political calculation seems applicable to the Soviet Union even within present data constraints. A systematic examination of the published output of contemporary Soviet leaders for evidence of continuity and change with respect to propositions about the classical Bolshevik "operational code" elaborated by Leites (1953, 1964) for the Leninist/Stalinist generation of leaders and later modified for the Khrushchev era would be a useful first step. Comparative studies of the "operational codes" of Soviet and other Communist leaderships should also now be possible and might be suggestive of future trends in the evolution of the world-views of the Soviet political elite.

Indirect evidence about leader beliefs may be gleaned from the study of the literature of some of the emerging social science disciplines in the USSR, though the degree of exposure of high level Soviet political leaders to academic "policy analysts" is conjectural.[102] "Elite studies" of the situational contexts of key decisionmakers should devote more attention to foreign policy issues.

Expanding professional and personal contacts between American Sovietologists and Soviet international relations specialists can also be expected to yield additional information to supplement published material. Petrov (1973) calls attention to members of Soviet international relations and American studies institutes as new sources of inputs to the foreign policy decisionmaking process in the USSR and speculates on substantive predispositions of these experts. A more systematic effort to assess the policy influence of the new breed of Soviet *institutchiki* and to integrate findings from the analysis of their published outputs and insights gained from direct professional contacts with them is warranted.

Case Studies

Case studies provide the indispensable foundation of established knowledge upon which any new theoretical approaches to the study of Soviet foreign policy decisionmaking will have to be built. But as noted in Sec. III, the Soviet foreign policy case study literature is thin and fragmentary. Its unsatisfactory state impedes cumulation and replication and is a basic obstacle to the desirable goal of encouraging competition among alternative approaches to decisionmaking analysis across a common set of cases. Ideally, with a large set of comprehensive historical-narrative case studies in hand, parallel studies of each case conducted by scholars employing alternative or competing analytical approaches might be undertaken. Such studies might, in turn, serve as the basis for an integrating, synthesizing effort at model-building. The explanatory potential of parallel "cuts" at a single case utilizing alternative conceptual schemes has been demonstrated by Allison (1971). Pendill (1969) has employed a single case to test alternative hypotheses about the influence

---

[101] Hough (1969, 1973) provides a rich analysis of Soviet organizational behavior at the level of the district party organization and considers the applicability to the USSR of various Western "models" of organizational behavior. Organizational behavior of Soviet enterprises receives attention in Granick (1954, 1973) and other managerial and economic studies.

[102] The best example to date of this approach is Zimmerman (1969).

of factional struggle on foreign policy formation. But these two efforts virtually exhaust this analytical genre in Soviet studies. *There are too few case studies of a sufficiently rich and comprehensive character now available to permit much further experimentation with competing alternative approaches.*

Unfortunately, the low probability of uncovering sufficient data from which to construct a reasonably complete or comprehensive case study has discouraged most academic researchers from making the attempt. Case studies have fallen between the stools of high level generalization based on fragmentary "case illustrations," on one hand, and intensive dissection of selected aspects of particular cases, on the other. *The professional incentive structure of the academic community tends to work against the production of case studies that are fated to be incomplete, inconclusive, partial contributions to the storehouse of cumulative general knowledge.*

There is one strikingly underutilized source of data on Soviet decisionmaking that might provide sufficiently rich materials to satisfy the requirements of the academic case study researcher. In almost all of the best case studies of U.S. foreign policy decisionmaking, the testimony of decisionmakers themselves (acquired through memoirs, interviews, etc.) constitutes the critical data base. The absence of this type of evidence is the single most important lacuna in Soviet data on post-war foreign policy decisionmaking.* But for a variety of reasons, including payment of political debts, the exigencies of de-Stalinization, self-glorification of current leaders, and indoctrination, the wartime years have become the subject of an extensive memoir literature, primarily by Soviet military leaders but also by diplomats, and detailed multivolume official histories are readily available. This literature has thus far not been systematically examined for the purpose of extracting from it materials for case studies of wartime military and foreign policy decisions.

Media-Leadership Linkages

Regardless of the conceptual framework and techniques employed for analyzing the conduct of Soviet foreign policy, the published and broadcast output of Soviet media is certain to remain the prime source of evidence for academic research in this field. Lacking more direct access to the Soviet policy process, analysts of differing conceptual persuasions and employing a variety of techniques are obliged to mine essentially the same body of media data for inferences bearing on Soviet decisionmaking. *Considerable ingenuity and sophistication have been demonstrated in the organization, measurement, and manipulation of data extracted from the Soviet press, but assumptions about the relationship between press materials and the political actors whose attitudes or behavior are inferred from them have rarely been subjected to careful or systematic scrutiny.* The standard inference pattern associates the output of a particular Soviet newspaper or journal with the organization publishing it, the organization with the leader at the top of the organizational pyramid, or (in the case of professional journals), with a particular specialized professional "interest group" (e.g., *Pravda,* = the CPSU Central Committee Party apparatchiks = the General Secretary). These assumptions are too crude and undifferentiated to support the weight of the far-reaching conclusions often drawn from them. For example, studies of the Soviet military establishment frequently focus on internal strains and tensions arising from the partly divergent interests of the "commissars" and the "military professionals," yet the military press organs *(Krasnaia Zvezda, Kommunist Vooruzhennykh Sil)* from which evidence of professional military attitudes and preferences is drawn in juxtaposition to the attitudes of "the Party," are

---

* The one outstanding exception is the transcript of Nikita Khrushchev's tape-recorded memoirs, translated and edited by Talbott (1970, 1974). Remarkably, Khrushchev's memoirs, the authenticity of which is no longer in dispute, have been little exploited in the analytical literature. Despite errors, distortions, and gaps, they are an incomparably rich source of data on high-level Soviet decisionmaking from the late 1930s to 1964.

published directly or supervised by the Main Political Administration of the Ministry of Defense, which functions as a department of the CPSU Central Committee.[103]

Systematic differences in patterns of output among Soviet press organs are undoubtedly of political significance. Analysis of such patterns is an indispensable tool for the study of Soviet decisionmaking. But understanding of the source/actor relationship lags behind the development of techniques for discovering and manipulating press output variables. *To improve the utility of policy inferences drawn from content analysis of the Soviet press, the imbalance between the high level of effort expended on refining techniques of content analysis, on the one hand, and the comparatively meager investment in basic studies of the press as vehicles of partisan political communication,[104] on the other, should be corrected.*

Organizational case studies of major Soviet press organs could contribute significantly toward this end. The career paths of past and present editors of major press organs and their intersections with those of top political leaders have not been traced. There are scattered references in the literature to the association of particular journalists with high level party leaders and to the periodic use in the Soviet press of pseudonyms for high level authors of particularly sensitive articles, but this information has not been collated or organized in a way that permits generalization.[105] A study of the editorial process examining standard operating procedures governing the commissioning, selection, and editing of press materials (particularly deviations from the norm, including extra-editorial board interventions) would be helpful. Former Soviet journalists and contributors to Soviet professional journals who have recently emigrated from the USSR are promising potential new sources of data for such research.[106]

Helpful analogies can probably be drawn from parallel studies of the use of East European press organs for partisan political communication; the data base for such studies (former editors and journalists now in the West) is much richer than in the Soviet case. For example, a study of the Czechoslovak press in 1966-1968 would illuminate how a part of it was transferred into indisputably "representative" organs of particular factions and groupings (at the same time indicating to what extent it had those attributes under Novotny). The Polish media could provide a useful study as to how a particular leadership faction (the "Partisans") came to secure control of specialized press organs (including *Prawo i Zycie* and *Zolnierz Wolnosci*, formally "professional" organs of the Lawyers' Association and the Political Administration of the Armed Forces, respectively).

To sum up, there is considerable room for improvement in the quality and relevance to the foreign policy analyst of research on the international behavior of the Soviet Union; models and insights derived from social science decision theory hold out promise for improving research performance, chiefly by providing multiple perspectives and contributing to more disciplined structuring of analysis and collection of data. But neither the present level of development of models derived from decision theory nor the state of established knowledge about the context of Soviet decisionmaking permit us to expect that dramatic improvements in Soviet foreign policy studies could be made through direct and immediate application of extant decisionmaking models. Soviet data constraints are severe; the degree of "fit" of the Soviet decisionmaking system into the theoretical framework

---

[103] Mackintosh (1973).

[104] Books on the Soviet media, including Buzek (1964) and Hopkins (1970), ignore the subject entirely.

[105] For example, there is no analysis in the literature of the class of special policy-sensitive *Pravda* commentaries signed with the pseudonym "I. Alexandrov."

[106] See, for example, the interview with a former correspondent of *Literaturnaia gazeta*, the organ of the Union of Soviet Writers (Radio Liberty Dispatch, July 9, 1973).

thus far elaborated is uncertain; and the task of operationalizing models of decision-making to render them more usable for the study of Soviet foreign policy still lies ahead. The most important immediate priorities are to improve and enlarge the established knowledge base about the context of Soviet foreign policy decisionmaking in ways that will render that knowledge more susceptible to disciplined inquiry; and to formulate and test decision theories in the middle range that are specific to what is known and can be learned about the Soviet decisionmaking context.

REFERENCES

ABELSON, Robert (1973): "The structure of belief systems," in (R. Schank and K. Colby, eds.) *Computer Models of Thought and Language,* W. H. Freeman, San Francisco.

ADOMEIT, Hannes Jurgen (in progress): *Risk Taking, Crisis, and Conflict Behavior in Soviet Foreign Policy After World War II: An Empirical and Theoretical Analysis,* Ph.D. dissertation, Department of Political Science, Columbia University, New York.

———— (1973): *Soviet Risk Taking and Crisis Behavior: From Confrontation to Coexistence,* International Institute of Strategic Studies, Adelphi Papers No. 101, London.

AHARONI, Yair (1966): *The Foreign Investment Decision Process,* Graduate School of Business Administration, Harvard University, Cambridge, Massachusetts.

ALEXANDER, Arthur J. (1970): *R&D in Soviet Aviation,* R-589-PR, The Rand Corporation, Santa Monica, California.

———— (1973): *Weapons Acquisition in the Soviet Union, United States, and France,* P-4989, The Rand Corporation, Santa Monica, California.

ALEXANDER, Christopher (1968): *Notes on the Synthesis of Form,* Harvard University Press, Cambridge, Massachusetts.

ALLISON, Graham (1971): *Essence of Decision,* Little, Brown, Boston.

ANGELL, Robert C., DUNHAM, Vera S., and SINGER, J. David (1964): "Social values and foreign policy attitudes of Soviet and American elites," *J. Conf. Res. 8,* 329-491.

ARDREY, Robert (1966): *The Territorial Imperative,* Atheneum, New York.

ARMACOST, Michael H. (1969): *The Politics of Weapons Acquisition: The Thor-Jupiter Controversy,* Columbia University Press, New York.

ARMSTRONG, John A. (1965a): "The domestic roots of Soviet foreign policy," *Int. Affairs 42,* 37-47; reprinted in Hoffmann and Fleron (1971), 50-60.

———— (1965b): "Sources of administrative behavior: some Soviet and Western European comparisons," *Amer. Pol. Sci. Rev. 59,* 643-655; reprinted in Fleron (1969a), 357-378.

———— (1962): *Ideology, Politics, and Government in the Soviet Union,* Praeger, New York.

ARROW, Kenneth (1961): *Social Choice and Individual Values,* John Wiley, New York.

ASHBY, W. Ross (1952): *A Design for a Brain,* John Wiley, New York.

———— (1970): *An Introduction to Cybernetics,* Chapman & Hall, London.

ASPATURIAN, Vernon V. (1958): "Ideology and national interest in Soviet foreign policy," in (R. C. Macridis, ed.) *Foreign Policy in World Politics,* Prentice-Hall, Englewood Cliffs, New Jersey; reprinted in Aspaturian (1971), 327-349.

———— (1959): "The Union Republics and Soviet diplomacy: concepts, institutions, and practices," *Amer. Pol. Sci. Rev. 53,* 383-411; reprinted in Aspaturian (1971), 666-698.

———— (1966): "Internal politics and foreign policy in the Soviet system," in (R. B. Farrell, ed.) *Approaches to Comparative and International Politics,* Northwestern University Press, Evanston, Illinois; reprinted in Aspaturian (1971), 491-551.

—— (1969): "Soviet foreign policy at the crossroads: conflict and/or collaboration?" *Int. Org. 23,* 589-620; reprinted in edited form in Aspaturian (1971), 915-939.

—— (1971): *Process and Power in Soviet Foreign Policy,* Little, Brown, Boston.

BALDWIN, David A. (1971): "The power of positive sanctions," *World Pol. 24,* 19-38.

BARBER, Benjamin R. (1969): "Conceptual foundations of totalitarianism," in (C. Friedrich, M. Curtis, and B. Barber, eds.) *Totalitarianism in Perspective: Three Views,* Praeger, New York.

BAUER, Raymond, INKELES, A., and KLUCKHOHN, C. K. (1956): *How the Soviet System Works: Cultural, Psychological and Social Themes,* Harvard University Press, Cambridge, Massachusetts.

BAUMOL, William J. (1952): *Welfare Economics and the Theory of the State,* Harvard University Press, Cambridge, Massachusetts.

—— (1972): *Economic Theory and Operations Analysis,* 3rd ed., Prentice-Hall, Englewood Cliffs, New Jersey.

BECK, Carl, FLERON, Frederic J., Jr., LODGE, Milton, WALLER, Derek J., WELSH, William A., and ZANINOVICH, M. George (1973): *Comparative Communist Political Leadership,* David McKay Company, New York.

BECKER, A. S., and HORELICK, A. L. (1970): *Soviet Policy in the Middle East,* R-504-FF, The Rand Corporation, Santa Monica, California.

BECKER, G. B., and McCLINTOCK, C. G. (1967): "Value: behavioral decision theory," *Annual Rev. of Psych. 18,* 239-286.

BEER, Stafford (1959): *Cybernetics and Management,* John Wiley, New York.

BELL, Coral (1971): *The Conventions of Crisis: A Study in Diplomatic Management,* Oxford University Press, London.

BELL, Daniel (1958): "Ten theories in search of reality: the prediction of Soviet behavior," *World Pol. 10,* 315-353; reprinted in Aspaturian (1971), 289-323.

—— (1964): "Twelve modes of prediction: a preliminary sorting of approaches in the social sciences," *Daedalus 93,* 845-880.

BELLMAN, Richard (1961): *Adaptive Control Processes,* Princeton University Press, Princeton, New Jersey.

BENEDICT, Ruth (1946): *The Chrysanthemum and the Sword: Patterns of Japanese Culture,* Houghton-Mifflin, Boston, Massachusetts.

BLACKMER, Donald L. (1968): "Scholars and policy-makers: perceptions of Soviet policy," paper prepared for the 1968 annual meeting of the American Political Science Association.

BLAU, Peter (1955): *The Dynamics of Bureaucracy,* University of Chicago Press, Chicago.

BLOOMFIELD, Lincoln P., and BEATTIE, Robert R. (1971): "Computers and policy making: the Cascon experiment," *J. Conf. Res. 15,* 33-53.

BLOOMFIELD, Lincoln P., Walter C. CLEMENS, and Franklyn GRIFFITHS, (1966): *Khrushchev and the Arms Race,* The M.I.T. Press, Cambridge, Massachusetts.

BLOOMFIELD, Lincoln P., and WHALEY, Barton (1965): "The political-military exercise: a progress report," *Orbis 8,* 854-870.

BORKENAU, Franz (1953): *European Communism,* Faber & Faber, London.

BOWER, Joseph L. (1970): *Managing the Resource Allocation Process,* Graduate School of Business Administration, Harvard University, Boston, Massachusetts.

BRAFF, A. J. (1969): *Microeconomic Analysis,* John Wiley, New York.

BRECHER, Michael, STEINBERG, Blema, and STEIN, Janice (1969): "A framework for research on foreign policy behavior," *J. Conf. Res. 13,* 75-101.

BREWER, Garry D., and HALL, Owen P., Jr. (1973): "Policy analysis by computer simulation: the need for appraisal," *Public Policy 21,* 343-365.

BRODY, Richard, and VESECKY, John (1969): "Soviet openness to changing situations: a critical evaluation of certain hypotheses about Soviet foreign policy behavior," in (J. Triska, ed.) *Communist Party-States: Comparative and International Studies,* Bobbs-Merrill, Indianapolis.

BRONFENBRENNER, Urie (1961): "Allowing for Soviet perceptions," *J. Social Issues 17,* 45-56; reprinted in Fisher (1964), 161-178.

BROWN, A. H. (1971): "Policy-making in the Soviet Union," *Sov. Studies 23,* 120-148.

——— (1972): "Problems of interest articulation and group influence in the Soviet Union (review of Skilling and Griffiths, *Interest Groups in Soviet Politics*)," *Gov. & Opposition 7,* 229-243.

BRUNNER, Ronald D., and LIEPELT, Klaus (1972): "Data analysis, process analysis, and system change," *Midwest. J. Pol. Sci. 16,* 538-569.

BRZEZINSKI, Zbigniew (1962): *Ideology and Power in Soviet Politics,* Praeger, New York.

——— (1967): *The Soviet Bloc: Unity and Conflict,* rev. ed., Harvard University Press, Cambridge, Massachusetts.

——— (1968): "Peace and power: looking toward the 1970s," *Encounter 31* (November), 3-13; reprinted in Aspaturian (1971), 863-878.

———, (1972): "The balance of power delusion," *For. Policy 7,* 54-59.

———, and HUNTINGTON, Samuel (1964): *Political Power: USA/USSR,* Viking Press, New York.

BUCHANAN, James N., and TULLOCH, Gordon (1967): *The Calculus of Consent: The Logical Foundation of Constitutional Democracy,* University of Michigan Press, Ann Arbor, Michigan.

BURKS, R. V. (ed.) (1968): *The Future of Communism in Europe,* Wayne State University Press, Detroit.

BUZEK, Antony (1964): *How the Communist Press Works,* Praeger, London.

CAMPBELL, Heather (1972): *Controversy in Soviet R&D: The Airship Case Study,* R-1001-PR, The Rand Corporation, Santa Monica.

CHANDLER, Alfred (1962): *Strategy and Structure,* MIT Press, Cambridge, Massachusetts.

CHANEY, Otto Preston, Jr. (1971): *Zhukov,* University of Oklahoma Press, Norman, Oklahoma.

CHOMSKY, Noam (1959): "Review of B. F. Skinner, *Verbal Behavior,*" *Language 35,* 26-58.

CHURCH, Nancy (1973): *The Kennedy Neurosis: A Psychological Portrait of an American Dynasty,* Grosset & Dunlop, New York.

CLEMENS, Walter C., Jr. (1966): "Underlying factors in Soviet arms control policy: problems of systematic analysis," in *Peace Research Society (International) Papers 6,* Vienna Conference, 1966, 51-70.

——— (1969): "Soviet policy in the Third World in the 1970's," *Orbis 13,* 476-501; reprinted in Hoffmann and Fleron (1971), 426-447.

CONQUEST, Robert (1961): *Power and Policy in the U.S.S.R.,* St. Martin's Press, New York.

——— (1963): "After Khrushchev: a conservative restoration?" *Probs. of Communism 12,* No. 5, 41-46.

COTTRELL, Alvin J. (1970): "The Soviet Union in the Middle East," *Orbis 14,* 588-598.

"The coup and after" (1965): a symposium, *Probs. of Communism 14,* No. 1, 1-31 (Part I): No. 3, 37-45 (Part II): No. 4, 72-76 (Part III).

CRECINE, John P. (1969): *Governmental Problem Solving,* Rand McNally, Chicago.

CURTIS, Michael (1971): "Soviet-American relations and the Middle East crisis," *Orbis 15,* 403-427.

CYERT, Richard M., and MARCH, James G. (1963): *A Behavioral Theory of the Firm,* Prentice-Hall, Englewood Cliffs, New Jersey.

DALLIN, Alexander (1960): *Soviet Conduct in World Affairs,* Columbia University Press, New York.

———, (1963): "Soviet Union: political activity," in (Z. Brzezinski, ed.) *Africa and the Communist World,* Stanford University Press, Stanford, California.

———, et al. (1964): *The Soviet Union, Arms Control, and Disarmament: A Study of Soviet Attitudes,* Columbia University Press, New York.

——— (1969): "Soviet foreign policy and domestic politics: a framework for analysis," *J. Int. Affairs 23,* 250-265; reprinted in Hoffmann and Fleron (1971), 36-49.

——— (1973): "Bias and blunders in American studies on the USSR," with comment by John A. Armstrong, *Slavic Rev. 32,* 560-587.

———, and WESTIN, Alan F. (1966): *Politics in the Soviet Union: 7 Cases,* Harcourt, Brace & World, New York.

DANIELS, Robert V. (1965): "Doctrine and foreign policy," *Survey 57,* 3-13; reprinted in Hoffmann and Fleron (1971), 154-164.

DAVIS, O. A., DEMPSTER, M. A., and WILDAVSKY, A. (1966): *On the Process of Budgeting: An Empirical Study of Congressional Appropriations,* Graduate School of Public Administration, Carnegie-Mellon University, Pittsburgh.

DAVISON, William P. (1958): *The Berlin Blockade,* Princeton University Press, Princeton, New Jersey.

DE RIVERA, Joseph H. (1968): *The Psychological Dimension of Foreign Policy,* Charles Merrill, Columbus, Ohio.

DEUTSCH, Karl (1960): "Toward an inventory of basic trends and patterns in comparative and international politics," *Amer. Pol. Sci. Rev. 54,* 34-57; reprinted in Rosenau (1969), 498-512.

——— (1963): *The Nerves of Government: Models for Political Communication and Control,* Free Press, New York.

———, and SINGER, J. David (1964): "Multipolar power systems and international stability," *World Pol. 16,* 390-406; reprinted in Rosenau (1969), 315-324.

DEUTSCHER, Isaac (1965): "Constellations of lobbies," *The Nation,* April 5, 1965, 352-357.

DINERSTEIN, Herbert S. (1968): *Fifty Years of Soviet Foreign Policy,* Johns Hopkins Press, Baltimore.

——— (1969): "Review of Adam B. Ulam, *Expansion and Coexistence,*" *Amer. Pol. Sci. Rev. 63,* 537-539.

DIVINE, Robert A. (ed.) (1971): *The Cuban Missile Crisis,* Quadrangle Books, Chicago.

DORFMAN, Robert (1964): *The Price System,* Prentice-Hall, Englewood Cliffs, New Jersey.

———, SAMUELSON, Paul, and SOLOW, Robert (1958): *Linear Programming and Economic Analysis,* McGraw-Hill, New York.

DOWNS, Anthony (1957): *An Economic Theory of Democracy,* Harper, New York.

——— (1967): *Inside Bureaucracy,* Little, Brown, Boston.

DRAPER, Theodore (1967): *Israel and World Politics,* Viking Press, New York.

ECKHARDT, William, and WHITE, Ralph K. (1967): "A test of the mirror-image hypothesis: Kennedy and Khrushchev," *J. Conf. Res. 11,) 325-332; reprinted in Hoffmann and Fleron (1971), 308-317.

EDINGER, Lewis J., and SEARING, Donald D. (1967): "Social background in elite analysis: a methodological inquiry," *Amer. Pol. Sci. Rev. 61,* 428-445.

EDWARDS, Ward (1954): "The theory of decision-making," *Psych. Bull. 51*, 380-417.
———— (1961): "Behavioral decision theory," *Annual Rev. of Psych. 12*, 473-498.
ENTHOVEN, Alain C., and SMITH, K. Wayne (1971): *How Much is Enough? Shaping the Defense Program, 1961-69*, Harper & Row, New York.
ERICKSON, John (1972): "Review of *New Trends in Kremlin Policy* and WESSON, R. G., *Soviet Foreign Policy in Perspective,*" *Survival 14*, 146-149.
ERIKSON, Erik (1950): *Childhood and Society,* Norton, New York.
———— (1958, 1962): *Young Man Luther,* Norton, New York.
———— (1959): *Identity and the Life Cycle,* Volume 1, No. 1, of *Psychological Issues,* International Universities Press, New York.
———— (1969): *Gandhi's Truth,* Norton, New York.
ERMARTH, Fritz (1969): *Internationalism, Security, and Legitimacy: The Challenge to Soviet Interests in East Europe, 1964-1968*, RM-5909-PR, The Rand Corporation, Santa Monica, California.
FAINSOD, Merle (1958): *Smolensk Under Soviet Rule,* Harvard University Press, Cambridge, Massachusetts.
FARQUHARSON, R. (1969): *Theory of Voting,* Yale University Press, New Haven, Connecticut.
FARRAR, L. L., Jr. (1972): "The limits of choice: July 1914 reconsidered," *J. Conf. Res. 14*, 1-23.
FARRELL, R. Barry (ed.) (1966): *Approaches to Comparative and International Politics,* Northwestern University Press, Evanston, Illinois.
———— (1970): *Political Leadership in Eastern Europe and the Soviet Union,* Aldine, Chicago.
FEDDER, Edwin H. (ed.) (1970): *Methodological Concerns in International Studies,* University of Missouri Press, St. Louis.
FENICHEL, Otto (1945): *The Psychoanalytic Theory of Neurosis,* Norton, New York.
———— (1968): "Soviet area studies and the social sciences: some methodological problems in Communist studies," *Sov. Studies 19*, 313-339.
FLERON, Frederic J., Jr. (ed.) (1969a): *Communist Studies and the Social Sciences,* Rand McNally, Chicago.
———— (1969b): "Co-optation as a mechanism of adaption to change: the Soviet political leadership system," *Polity 2*, 176-201; reprinted in Kanet (1971), 125-149.
———— (1969c): "Research strategies for the study of Communist systems," *Can. Slavic Studies 3*, 544-552.
———— (1970): "Representation of career types in the Soviet political leadership," in (R. B. Farrell, ed.) *Political Leadership in Eastern Europe and the Soviet Union,* Aldine, Chicago.
FRANCK, Thomas M., and WEISBAND, Edward (1971): *Word Politics: Verbal Strategy Among the Superpowers,* Oxford University Press, New York.
FRANK, Peter (1972): "Review of Michael P. Gehlen, *The Communist Party of the Soviet Union: A Functional Analysis,*" *Sov. Studies 23*, 672-674.
FRANKEL, Joseph (1963): *The Making of Foreign Policy: An Analysis of Decision-Making,* Oxford University Press, London.
FREUD, Anna (1946): *The Ego and Mechanisms of Defense,* International University Press, New York.
———— (1948): *Group Psychology and the Analysis of the Ego,* Hogarth Press, London.
FREUD, Sigmund (1960): *A General Introduction to Psychoanalysis,* Washington Square Press, New York.

FRIEDRICH, Carl, CURTIS, Michael, and BARBER, Benjamin (1969): *Totalitarianism in Perspective: Three Views,* Praeger, New York.

"Further on the leadership" (1972): *Sov. Analyst 1,* November 2, 1-3.

GALLAGHER, Matthew P., and SPIELMANN, Karl F., Jr. (1972): *Soviet Decision-Making for Defense: A Critique of U.S. Perspectives on the Arms Race,* Praeger, New York.

GALTUNG, Johan (1966): "East-West interaction patterns," *J. Peace Res. 2,* 146-177.

GAMSON, William A., and MODIGLIANI, Andre (1968): "Some aspects of Soviet-Western conflict," *Peace Research Society (International) Papers,* No. 9, 9-24.

——— (1971): *Untangling the Cold War,* Little, Brown, Boston.

GATI, Charles (1970): "History, social science, and the study of Soviet foreign policy," *Slavic Rev. 29,* 682-687; reprinted in Hoffmann and Fleron (1971), 11-17.

——— (1971): "Soviet elite perception of international regions: a research note," in (R. E. Kanet, ed.) *The Behavioral Revolution and Communist Studies,* Free Press, New York.

———, KANET, Roger E., KRISCH, Henry, and FINLEY, David O. (1971): "The comparative study of Communist foreign policies," symposium at the Northeastern Slavic Conference, American Association for the Advancement of Slavic Studies, Montreal, Canada.

GEHLEN, Michael P. (1965): "Group theory and the study of Soviet politics," in (S. I. Ploss, ed.) *Conflict and Decision-Making in the Soviet Union,* Princeton University Press, Princeton, New Jersey.

——— (1967): *The Politics of Coexistence: Soviet Methods and Motives,* Indiana University, Bloomington.

———, and McBRIDE, Michael (1968): "The Soviet Central Committee: an elite analysis," *Amer. Pol. Sci. Rev. 62,* 1232-1241; reprinted in Kanet (1971), 103-124.

GEORGE, Alexander L. (1969): "The 'operational code': a neglected approach to the study of political leaders and decision-making," *Int. Studies Q. 8,* 190-222; reprinted in Hoffmann and Fleron (1971), 165-190.

———, and GEORGE, Juliette (1956): *Woodrow Wilson and Colonel House: A Personality Study,* John Day, New York.

GEORGE, Alexander L., HALL, David K., and SIMONS, William R. (1971): *The Limits of Coercive Diplomacy,* Little, Brown, Boston.

GIFFIN, Sidney (1965): *The Crisis Game: Simulating International Conflict,* Doubleday, New York.

GLASER, William A. (1956): "Theories of Soviet foreign policy: a classification of the literature," *World Aff. Q. 27,* 128-152.

GLASSMAN, Jon D. (1968): "Soviet foreign policy decision-making," in *Columbia Essays in International Affairs: Volume III, The Dean's Papers, 1967,* Columbia University Press, New York, 373-402.

GOLEMBIEWSKI, Robert T., WELSH, William A., and CROTTY, William J. (1969): *A Methodological Primer for Political Scientists,* Rand McNally, Chicago.

GORMAN, Robert A. (1970): "On the inadequacies of non-philosophical political science: a critical analysis of decision-making theory," *Int. Studies Q. 14.,* 395-411.

GRANICK, David (1954): *Management of the Industrial Firm in the USSR,* Columbia University Press, New York.

——— (1973): "Managerial incentives in the USSR and in Western firms; implications for behavior," *J. Compar. Admin. 5,* 134-168.

GRIFFITH, William E. (1964): *The Sino-Soviet Rift*, MIT Press, Cambridge, Massachusetts.

GURR, Ted R. (1970): *Why Men Rebel*, Princeton University Press, Princeton, New Jersey.

HAAS, Michael, and KARIEL, Henry S. (1970): *Approaches to the Study of Political Science*, Chandler, Scranton, Pennsylvania.

HALL, Calvin S. (1954): *A Primer of Freudian Psychology*, Mentor Books, New York.

HALPER, Thomas (1971): *Foreign Policy Crises: Appearance and Reality in Decision-Making*, Merrill, Columbus, Ohio.

HALPERIN, Morton H. (ed.) (1967): *Sino-Soviet Relations and Arms Control*, MIT Press, Cambridge, Massachusetts.

—— (1974): *Bureaucratic Politics and Foreign Policy*, The Brookings Institution, Washington, D.C.

——, and KANTOR, Arnold (eds.) (1973): *Readings in American Foreign Policy: The Bureaucratic Perspective*, Little, Brown, Boston.

HAVEMAN, Robert H., and MARGOLIS, Julius (eds.) (1970): *Public Expenditures and Policy Analysis*, Markham, Chicago.

HELDMAN, Dan C. (1971): "Soviet relations with the developing states: an application of correlation analysis," in Kanet (1971), 339-363.

HERMANN, Charles F. (1968): "The comparative study of foreign policy," *World Pol. 20*, 521-534.

—— (1969a): *Crises in Foreign Policy*, Bobbs-Merrill, Indianapolis.

——, (1969b): "International crisis as a situational variable," in Rosenau (1969), 409-421.

—— (ed.) (1972): *International Crises*, Free Press, New York.

——, and HERMANN, Margaret (1967): "An attempt to simulate the outbreak of World War I," *Amer. Pol. Sci. Rev. 61*, 400-416; reprinted in Rosenau (1969), 622-639.

HILSMAN, Roger (1967): *To Move a Nation*, Doubleday, New York.

HIRSCH, P., and LEITES, Nathan (1969): "A sketch of debolshevization at the top: changes of orientation in the leadership of a ruling Communist Party seen through public statements: the spring of 1968 in Czechoslovakia," draft manuscript, The Rand Corporation, Santa Monica, California.

HITCH, C. J., and McKEAN, R. (1965): *The Economics of Defense in the Nuclear Age*, Atheneum, New York.

HODGSON, John H. (1971): "Soviet foreign policy: mental alienation or universal revolution?" *West. Pol. Q. 24*, 653-665.

HODNETT, Grey, and POTICHNYJ, Peter J. (1970): "The Ukraine and the Czechoslovak crisis," Occasional Paper No. 6, Department of Political Science, Research School of Social Sciences, Australian National University, Canberra.

HOFFMANN, Erik P. (1969): "Methodological problems of Kremlinology," in (F. J. Fleron, Jr., ed.) *Communist Studies and the Social Sciences*, Rand McNally, Chicago, 129-149.

—— (1971): "Role conflict and ambiguity in the Communist Party of the Soviet Union," in (R. E. Kanet, ed.) *The Behavioral Revolution in Communist Studies*, Free Press, New York, 233-258.

—— (1972): "Social science and Soviet administrative behavior; a review of Jerry F. Hough, *The Soviet Prefects*," *World Pol. 24*, 444-471.

——, and FLERON, Frederic J., Jr., (eds.) (1971): *The Conduct of Soviet Foreign Policy*, Aldine-Atherton, Chicago.

HOLSTI, K. J. (1970): "National role conceptions in the study of foreign policy," *Int. Studies Q. 14*, 233-309.

HOLSTI, Ole R. (1971): "Crisis, stress and decision-making," *Int. Social Sci. J. 23*, 53-67.

—— (1972a): *Crisis Escalation War,* McGill-Queen's University Press, Montreal.

—— (1972b): "Review of Graham T. Allison, *Essence of Decision,*" *West. Pol. Q. 25*, 136-140.

——, BRODY, Richard A., and NORTH, Robert C. (1964): "The management of international crisis: affect and action in American-Soviet relations," *J. Peace Res. 3-4*, 170-190; reprinted in Pruitt and Snyder (1969), 62-79.

HOPKINS, Mark W. (1970): *Mass Media in the Soviet Union,* Pegasus, New York.

HOPMANN, P. Terrence (1967): "International conflict and cohesion in the Communist system," *Int. Studies Q.,* 212-236; reprinted, revised, and enlarged in Kanet (1971), 301-338.

HORELICK, Arnold (1964): "The Cuban missile crisis: an analysis of Soviet calculations and behavior," *World Pol. 16,* 363-389; reprinted in Hoffmann and Fleron (1971), 346-370.

—— (1968): "Fifty years after October," in (R. V. Burks, ed.) *The Future of Communism in Europe,* Wayne State University Press, Detroit, 141-183.

——, and RUSH, Myron (1966): *Strategic Power and Soviet Foreign Policy,* University of Chicago Press, Chicago.

HORN, Robert C. (1972): "Perceptions of Soviet foreign policy," *Orbis 91,* 816-821.

HOROWITZ, Irving Louis (ed.) (1971): *The Use and Abuse of Social Science,* E. P. Dutton, New Brunswick, New Jersey.

HOUGH, Jerry F. (1969): *The Soviet Prefects: The Local Party Organs in Industrial Decision-Making,* Harvard University Press, Cambridge.

—— (1973): "The bureaucratic model and the nature of the Soviet system," *J. Compar. Admin. 5,* 134-168.

"How strong is Khrushchev?" (1963): *Probs. Communism 12,* No. 5, 27-46 (Part I); No. 6, 56-65 (Part II).

HUGHES, Barry, and VOLGY, Thomas (1970): "Distance in foreign policy behavior: a comparative study of Eastern Europe," *Midwest J. Pol. Sci. 16,* 459-492.

HUNTER, Douglas E. (1972): "Some aspects of a decision-making model in nuclear deterrence theory," *J. Peace Res.,* 209-222.

HUNTINGTON, Samuel P. (1961): *The Common Defense,* Columbia University Press, New York.

—— and MOORE, Clement H. (1970): *Authoritarian Politics in Modern Society,* Basic Books, New York.

HUTCHINGS, Raymond (1971): "Soviet defense spending and Soviet external relations," *Int. Affairs 47,* 518-531.

HYLAND, William, and SHRYOCK, Richard Wallace (1968): *The Fall of Khrushchev,* Funk & Wagnalls, New York.

"Ideology and power politics: a symposium," (1958): *Probs. of Communism 7,* No. 2, 10-30 and No. 3, 50-52; reprinted in Hoffmann and Fleron (1971), 101-135.

IKLÉ, Fred C. (1964): *How Nations Negotiate,* Harper, New York.

—— (1971): *Every War Must End,* Columbia University Press, New York.

JACOBSEN, C. C. (1972): *Soviet Strategy—Soviet Foreign Policy: Military Considerations Affecting Soviet Policy-Making,* University Press, Glasgow.

JACOBSON, Harold Karan, and ZIMMERMAN, William (eds.) (1969): *The Shaping of Foreign Policy,* Atherton Press, New York.

JAMES, Robert Rhodes (ed.) (1969): *The Czechoslovak Crisis 1968,* Weidenfeld & Nicolson, London.

JANDA, Kenneth (1969): *Data Processing: Applications to Political Research,* 2nd ed., Northwestern University Press, Evanston, Illinois.

JANIS, Irving L. (1972): *Victims of Groupthink: A Psychological Study of Foreign-Policy Decisions and Fiascoes,* Houghton-Mifflin, Boston.

JENSEN, Lloyd (1972): "Predicting international events," *Peace Res. Rev. 4,* No. 6, 1-66.

JERVIS, Robert (1967): "The costs of the scientific study of politics: an examination of the Stanford Content Analysis Studies," *Int. Studies Q. 9,* 366-393; reprinted and revised in Knorr and Rosenau (1969), 177-217.

———— (1968): "Hypotheses on misperception," *World Pol. 20,* 454-479.

———— (1970): *The Logic of Images in International Relations,* Princeton University Press, Princeton, New Jersey.

JOHNSON, A. Ross (1970): "Poland: end of an era?" *Probs. of Communism 19,* No. 1, 28-40.

JOHNSON, Chalmers (1970): *Change in Communist Systems,* Stanford University Press, Stanford, California.

JONES, Susan D., and SINGER, J. David (1972): *Beyond Conjecture in International Politics,* F. E. Peacock, Itasca, Illinois.

JÖNSSON, Christer (1972a): The Soviet Union and the test ban: a study in Soviet negotiating behavior, University of Lund (mimeo).

———— (ed.) (1972b): *Sovjets utrikespolitik (Soviet Foreign Policy),* Studentlitteratur, Lund.

JUVILER, Peter H., and MORTON, Henry W., (eds.) (1967): *Soviet Policy Making,* Praeger, New York.

KAHN, Herman (1961): *On Thermonuclear War,* Princeton University Press, Princeton, New Jersey.

KANET, Roger E. (1969): "Review of Jan F. Triska and David D. Finley, *Soviet Foreign Policy,*" *Orbis 12,* 937-940.

———— (ed.) (1971): *The Behavioral Revolution and Communist Studies,* Free Press, New York.

KAPLAN, Abraham (1964): *The Conduct of Inquiry: Methodology for Behavioral Science,* Chandler, San Francisco.

KASSOF, Allen (1968): *Prospects for Soviet Society,* Praeger, New York.

KELLY, Rita M., and FLERON, Frederic J., Jr. (1970): "Personality, behavior, and Communist ideology," *Sov. Studies,* 297-313; reprinted and enlarged in Hoffmann and Fleron (1971), 191-211; reprinted in Kanet (1971), 53-77.

KELMAN, Herbert C. (ed.) (1965): *International Behavior,* Holt, Rinehart & Winston, New York.

———— (1970): "The role of the individual in international relations: some conceptual and methodological considerations," *J. of Int. Affairs 24,* 1-17.

KENNAN, George F. (1961): *Russia and the West Under Lenin and Stalin,* Little, Brown, Boston.

KIMBLE, G. A. (ed.) (1961): *Hilgard and Marquis' Conditioning and Learning,* 2nd ed., Appleton-Century-Crofts, New York.

KINTNER, William R., and KLAIBER, Wolfgang (1971): *Eastern Europe and European Security,* Dunellen, New York.

————, and SCOTT, Harriet Fast (1968): *The Nuclear Revolution in Soviet Military Affairs,* University of Oklahoma Press, Norman, Oklahoma.

KNORR, Klaus, and ROSENAU, James N. (eds.) (1969): *Contending Approaches to International Politics,* Princeton University Press, Princeton, New Jersey.

KOLKOWICZ, Roman (1967): *The Soviet Military and the Communist Party,* Princeton University Press, Princeton, New Jersey.

KOOPMANS, T. C. (1957): *Three Essays on the State of Economic Science,* McGraw-Hill, New York.

KRANTZ, D. H., LUCE, R. D., SUPPES, P., and TVERSKY, A. (1971): *Foundations of Measurement. Volume 1: Additive and Polynomial Presentations,* Academic Press, New York.

KRASMER, Stephen D. (1972): "Are Bureaucracies Important? (Or Allison Wonderland)," *Foreign Policy,* No. 7, 159-179.

"Kremlinology" (1964): a symposium, *Survey 50,* 154-194.

KUHN, Thomas (1963): *The Structure of Scientific Revolutions,* University of Chicago Press, Chicago.

KULSI, Wladyslaw W. (1959): *Peaceful Coexistence: An Analysis of Soviet Foreign Policy,* Henry Regnery, Chicago.

LANE, David (1972): "Review of H. Gordon Skilling and Franklyn Griffiths (eds.), *Interest Groups in Soviet Politics,"* *Sov. Studies 23,* 668-672.

LANGER, Walter C. (1972): *The Mind of Adolf Hitler,* Basic Books, New York.

LANGSAM, David E., and PAUL, David W. (1972): "Soviet politics and the group approach: a conceptual note," *Slavic Rev. 31,* 136-141.

LAQUEUR, Walter (1959): *The Soviet Union and the Middle East,* Praeger, New York.

——— (1968): *The Road to Jerusalem: The Origins of the Arab-Israeli Conflict, 1967,* MacMillan, New York.

——— (1969): *The Struggle for the Middle East: The Soviet Union in the Mediterranean 1956-1968,* MacMillan, New York.

LASSWELL, Harold D. (1930): *Psychopathology and Politics,* University of Chicago Press, Chicago.

LEITES, Nathan (1951): *The Operational Code of the Politburo,* McGraw-Hill, New York.

——— (1953): *A Study of Bolshevism,* Free Press, Glencoe, Illinois.

——— (1963): *Kremlin Thoughts: Yielding, Rebuffing, Provoking, Retreating,* RM-3618-ISA, The Rand Corporation, Santa Monica, California.

——— (1964): *Kremlin Moods,* RM-3535-ISA, The Rand Corporation, Santa Monica, California.

LEONHARD, Wolfgang (1962): *The Kremlin Since Stalin,* Oxford University Press, London.

——— (1963): "An anti-Khrushchev opposition?" *Probs. of Communism 12,* No. 6, 61-64.

LERNER, Daniel (ed.) (1959): *The Human Meaning of the Social Sciences,* Meridian Books, New York.

LIAO, Kuang-sheng, and WHITING, Allen S. (1973): "Chinese press perceptions of threat: the U.S. and India, 1962," *China Q. 53,* 80-97.

LINDBLOM, Charles E. (1959): "The science of muddling through," *Public Admin. Rev. 19,* 79-88.

——— (1965): *The Intelligence of Democracy,* Free Press, New York.

LINDEN, Carl (1966a): "Khrushchev and the party battle," *Probs. of Communism 12,* No. 5, 27-35.

——— (1966b): *Khrushchev and the Soviet Leadership, 1957-1964,* Johns Hopkins Press, Baltimore.

LODGE, Milton C. (1969): *Soviet Elite Attitudes Since Stalin,* Bell & Howell, Columbus, Ohio.

LORENZ, Konrad (1966): *On Aggression,* Harcourt, Brace & World, New York.

LOWENTHAL, Abraham (1972): *The Dominican Intervention,* Harvard University Press, Cambridge, Massachusetts.

LOWENTHAL, Richard (1960): "Ideology, power and welfare," commentary for symposium "Toward a 'Communist welfare state'?" *Probs. of Communism 9,* No. 1, 18-21.

———— (1968): "The sparrow in the cage," *Probs. of Communism 17,* No. 6, 2-28.

LUCE, R. D., and RAIFFA, H. E. (1957): *Games and Decisions,* John Wiley, New York.

LUCE, R. D., and SUPPES, P. (1965): "Preference, utility, and subjective probability," in (R. P. Luce, R. R. Bush, and E. Galanter, eds.) *Handbook of Mathematical Psychology,* John Wiley, New York.

LYDEN, Fremont G., and MILLER, Ernest G. (1968): *Planning Programming and Budgeting: A Systems Approach to Management,* Markham, Chicago.

MACKINTOSH, J. M. (1962): *Strategy and Tactics of Soviet Foreign Policy,* Oxford University Press, London.

———— (1973): "The Soviet military: influence on foreign policy," *Probs. of Communism 22,* No. 5, 1-11.

MARCH, James G. (1965): *Handbook of Organizations,* Rand McNally, Chicago.

————, and SIMON, Herbert A. (1958): *Organizations,* John Wiley, New York.

MARKO, Kurt (1968): "Soviet ideology and Sovietology," *Sov. Studies 19,* 465-481.

MARSHALL, A. W. (1966): *Problems of Estimating Military Power,* P-3417, The Rand Corporation, Santa Monica, California.

———— (1971): "Bureaucratic behavior and the strategic arms competition," research paper published by the Southern California Arms Control and Foreign Policy Seminar, Santa Monica, California.

MAY, Ernest (1973): *Lessons of History: The Use and Misuse of History in American Foreign Policy,* Oxford University Press, New York.

MAZLISH, Bruce (1972): *In Search of Nixon: A Psychohistorical Inquiry,* Basic Books, New York.

McCLELLAND, Charles (1961): "The acute international crisis," *World Pol. 14,* 182-204.

———— (1962): "Decisional opportunity and political controversy: the Quemoy case," *J. Conf. Res. 6,* 201-212.

McKEAN, R. N. (1958): *Efficiency in Government through Systems Analysis with Emphasis on Water Resources Development,* John Wiley, New York.

MERRITT, Richard C., and ROKKAN, Stein (1966): *Comparing Nations,* Yale University Press, New Haven, Connecticut.

MEYER, Alfred G. (1965): *The Soviet Political System: An Interpretation,* Random House, New York.

MICHALAK, Stanley J., Jr. (1973): "Will the methodology of science resolve the continuing debate over Soviet external conduct?" *News. on Compar. Studies of Communism 6,* No. 2, 14-31.

MILES, Edward L., and GILLOOLY, John S. (1965): "Processes of interaction among the fourteen Communist Party states: an exploratory essay," *Stanford Studies of the Communist System,* Research Paper No. 5, Stanford University, Stanford, California.

MILLIKAN, Max F. (1959): "Inquiry and policy: the relation of knowledge to action," in (D. Lerner, ed.) *The Human Meaning of the Social Sciences,* Meridian Books, New York, 158-180.

MOROZOW, M. (1971): *Das sowjetische Establishment,* Seewald, Stuttgart.

MORSE, Philip M., and KIMBALL, George E. (1951): *Methods of Operations Research,* MIT Press, Cambridge, Massachusetts.

NAGEL, Ernest (1961): *The Structure of Science,* Harcourt & Brace, New York.

NATHAN, Andrew J. (1973): "The factionalism model for CCP politics," *China Q. 53,* 34-66.

NEAL, Fred Warner, and HAMLETT, Bruce D. (1969): "The never-never land of international relations," *Int. Studies Q. 13,* 281-305.

NEISSER, Ulric (1967): *Cognitive Psychology,* Appleton-Century-Crofts, New York.

NEUSTADT, Richard E. (1960): *Presidential Power: The Politics of Leadership,* John Wiley, New York.

—— (1970): *Alliance Politics,* Columbia University Press, New York.

New Trends in Kremlin Policy (1970): Special Report Series No. 11, Center for Strategic and International Studies, Georgetown University, Washington, D.C.

NEWELL, Allen, and SIMON, Herbert A. (1972): *Human Problem Solving,* Prentice-Hall, Englewood Cliffs, New Jersey.

NEWHOUSE, John (1973): *Cold Dawn: The Story of SALT,* Holt, Rinehart & Winston, New York.

NICOLAEVSKY, Boris I. (1953): "The meaning of the Beria Affair," *Novoe Russkoye Slovo* (December); reprinted in Nicolaevsky (1965), 130-147.

—— (1965): *Power and the Soviet Elite* (J. D. Zagoria, ed.), Praeger, New York.

NORTH, Robert C., HOLSTI, Ole R., ZANINOVICH, M. George, and ZINNES, Dina A. (1963): *Content Analysis,* Northwestern University Press, Evanston, Illinois.

NOVICK, D. (ed.) (1965): *Program Budgeting,* Harvard University Press, Cambridge, Massachusetts.

ODOM, William E. (1973): "The Soviet military; the Party connection," *Probs. of Communism 22 No. 5,* 12-26.

OLSON, Mancur (1965): *The Logic of Collective Action,* Harvard University Press, Cambridge, Massachusetts.

PACHTER, Henry M. (1963): *Collision Course: The Cuban Missile Crisis and Coexistence,* Praeger, New York.

PAIGE, Glenn D. (1968): *The Korean Decison,* Free Press, New York.

PAUL, David W. (1971): "Soviet foreign policy and the invasion of Czechoslovakia: a theory and a case study," *Int. Studies Q. 15,* 159-202.

PENDILL, C. Grant, Jr. (1969): *Foreign Policy and Political Factions in the USSR, 1952-1956: The Post-Stalin Power Struggle and the Developing Nations,* Ph.D. dissertation, University of Pennsylvania; summary version in Hoffmann and Fleron (1971), 61-75.

PENNOCK, J. Roland, and CHAPMAN, John W. (eds.) (1972): *Coercion, Nomos 14,* Aldine, Chicago.

PETHYBRIDGE, Roger (1962): *A Key to Soviet Politics: The Crisis of the Anti-Party Group,* Praeger, New York.

PETROV, Vladimir (1973): Formation of Soviet foreign policy," *Orbis 17,* 819-850.

PIPES, Richard (1973): "Operational principles of Soviet foreign policy," *Survey 19,* No. 2, 41-61.

PLOSS, Sidney I. (1965): *Conflict and Decision-Making in the Soviet Union: A Case Study of Agricultural Policy, 1953-1963,* Princeton University Press, Princeton, New Jersey.

—— (1967): "Studying the domestic determinants of Soviet foreign policy," *Can. Slavic Studies 1,* 44-59; reprinted in Hoffmann and Fleron (1971), 76-90.

—— (1968): "Interest groups," in (A. Kassof, ed.) *Prospects for Soviet Society,* Praeger, New York.

—— (ed.) (1971): *The Soviet Political Process: Aims, Techniques, and Examples of Analysis,* Ginn, Waltham, Massachusetts.

POOL, Ithiel de Sola (1952): *The "prestige papers": a survey of their editorials,* Stanford University Press, Stanford, California.

—— (ed.) (1959): *Trends in Content Analysis,* University of Illinois Press, Urbana.

—— (1960): "Content analysis for intelligence purposes," *World Pol. 12,* 478-485.

—— (1963): *Social Science Research and National Security,* Smithsonian Institute, Washington, D.C.

—— (1972): "International intelligence and domestic politics," in (Richard H. Blum, ed.), *Surveillance and Espionage in a Free Society: A Report by the Planning Group on Intelligence and Security to the Policy Council of the Democratic National Committee,* Praeger, New York, 272-297.

——, and KESSLER, Allen (1965): "The Kaiser, Tsar, and the computer: information processing in a crisis," *Amer. Behav. Scientist 8,* 31-38.

PRUITT, Dean G., and SNYDER, Richard C. (eds.) (1969): *Theory and Research on the Causes of War,* Prentice-Hall, Englewood Cliffs, New Jersey.

PYE, Lucian (1962): *Politics, Personality, and Nation Building: Burma's Search for Identity,* Yale University Press, New Haven, Connecticut.

——, and VERBA, Sidney (1965): *Political Culture and Political Development,* Princeton University Press, Princeton, New Jersey.

QUADE, E. S. (1964): *Analysis for Military Decisions,* Rand McNally, Chicago.

QUESTER, George (1966): *Deterrence Before Hiroshima,* John Wiley, New York.

RA'ANAN, Uri (1969): *The USSR Arms the Third World: Case Studies in Soviet Foreign Policy,* MIT Press, Cambridge, Massachusetts.

—— (1973): "The USSR and the Middle East: some reflections on the Soviet decision-making process," *Orbis 17,* 946-947.

RAIFFA, Howard (1968): *Decision Analysis,* Addison-Wesley, Reading, Massachusetts.

RANNEY, Austin (ed.) (1968): *Political Science and Public Policy,* Markham, Chicago.

RAPOPORT, Anatol (1971): *The Big Two: Soviet-American Perceptions of Foreign Policy,* Pegasus, New York.

——, and WALLSTEN, T. S. (1972): "Individual decision behavior," *Annual Rev. of Psych. 22,* 131-176.

REITMAN, W. (1965): *Cognition and Thought,* John Wiley, New York.

REMINGTON, Robin Alison (1971): *The Warsaw Pact: Case Studies in Communist Conflict Resolution,* MIT Press, Cambridge, Massachusetts.

RESHETAR, John S. (1955): *Problems of Analyzing and Predicting Soviet Behavior,* Doubleday, New York.

—— (1972): *The Soviet Polity: Government and Politics in the USSR,* Dodd, Mead, New York.

RIGBY, Thomas H. (1963): "The extent and limits of authority (a rejoinder to Mr. Linden)," *Probs. of Communism 12,* No. 5, 36-41.

—— (1970): "New trends in the study of Soviet politics," *Politics 5,* 1-17.

RIGGS, Douglas S. (1970): *Control Theory and Physiological Feedback Mechanisms,* Williams & Witkins, Baltimore.

RIKER, W. (1961): "Voting and the summation of preferences: an interpretive bibliographic review of selected developments during the last decade," *Amer. Pol. Sci. Rev. 55,* 900-911.

—— (1962): *The Theory of Political Coalitions,* Yale University Press, New Haven, Connecticut.

ROSENAU, James N. (ed.) (1967): *Domestic Sources of Foreign Policy,* Free Press, New York.

—— (1968): "Comparative foreign policy: fad, fantasy, or field?" *Int. Studies Q. 12,* 296-329.

—— (ed.) (1969): *International Politics and Foreign Policy,* rev. ed., Free Press, New York.

—— (1970): "Foreign policy as adaptive behavior: some preliminary notes for a theoretical model," *Compar. Politics 2,* 365-387.

ROTHENBERG, Jerome (1961): *The Measurement of Social Welfare,* Prentice-Hall, Englewood Cliffs, New Jersey.

RUBINSTEIN, Alvin Z. (1972): *The Foreign Policy of the Soviet Union,* 3rd ed., Random House, New York.

RUMMEL, Rudolf J. (1966): "Some dimensions in the foreign behavior of nations," *J. of Peace Res. 3,* 201-223; reprinted in Rosenau (1969), 600-621.

RUSH, Myron (1958): *The Rise of Khrushchev,* Public Affairs Press, Washington, D.C.

RYAVEC, Karl W. (1973): "Kremlinology or behavioralism?" *Probs. of Communism 22,* No. 1, 81-85.

SAMUELSON, Paul A. (1954): "The pure theory of public expenditure," *Rev. of Econ. & Stat. 36,* 387-389.

—— (1970): *Economics,* McGraw-Hill, New York.

SAPOLSKY, Harvey (1973): *The Polaris System Development: Bureaucratic Success in Government,* Harvard University Press, Cambridge, Massachusetts.

SARTORI, Giovanni (1970): "Concept misformation in comparative politics," *Amer. Pol. Sci. Rev. 64,* 1033-1053.

SAVAGE, L. J. (1959): *The Foundations of Statistics,* John Wiley, New York.

SCHELLING, Thomas C. (1960): *The Strategy of Conflict,* Harvard University Press, Cambridge, Massachusetts.

—— (1966): *Arms and Influence,* Yale University Press, New Haven, Connecticut.

SCHICK, Jack M. (1971): *The Berlin Crisis, 1958-1962,* University of Pennsylvania Press, Philadelphia.

SCHRODER, Harold, DRIVER, Michael, and STREUFERT, Siegfried (1967): *Human Information Processing,* Holt, Rinehart & Winston, New York.

SCHULTZE, C. (1968): *The Politics and Economics of Public Spending,* The Brookings Institution, Washington.

SCHWARTZ, David C. (1967): "Decision theories and crisis behavior: an empirical study of nuclear deterrence in international political crises," *Orbis 11,* 459-490.

SCHWARTZ, Joel, and KEECH, William R. (1968): "Group influence and the policy process in the Soviet Union," *Amer. Pol. Sci. Rev. 62,* 840-851; reprinted in Fleron (1969a), 298-317.

SHAPLEY, L. S., and SHUBIK, M. (1971): *Game Theory in Economics, Chapter 1: Introduction. The Use of Models,* R-904/1-NSF, The Rand Corporation, Santa Monica, California.

—— (1972a): *Game Theory in Economics, Chapter 2: Decisionmakers,* R-904/2-NSF, The Rand Corporation, Santa Monica, California.

—— (1972b): *Game Theory in Economics—Chapter 3: The "Rules of the Game,"* R-904/3-NSF, The Rand Corporation, Santa Monica, California.

—— (1973): *Game Theory in Economics—Chapter 6: Characteristic Function, Core, and Stable Set,* R-904/6-NSF, The Rand Corporation, Santa Monica, California.

SHARP, Samuel L. (1973): "Coexistence or consensus in American views of Soviet foreign policy," *Newsl. on Compar. Studies of Communism 6,* No. 2, 3-13.

SHUB, Anatole (1969): "Lessons of Czechoslovakia," *For. Affairs 47,* 266-280.

SHUBIK, Martin, and BREWER, Garry D. (1972a): *Models, Simulations, and Games—A Survey,* R-1060-ARPA/RC, The Rand Corporation, Santa Monica, California.

—— (1972b): *Reviews of Selected Books and Articles on Gaming and Simulation,* R-732-ARPA, The Rand Corporation, Santa Monica, California.

——, and SAVAGE, E. (1972): *The Literature of Gaming, Simulation and Model Building: Index and Critical Abstracts,* R-620-ARPA, The Rand Corporation, Santa Monica, California.

SHULMAN, Marshall (1966): *Beyond the Cold War,* Yale University Press, New Haven.
——— (1968): "Recent Soviet foreign policy: some patterns in retrospect," *J. of Int. Affairs 22,* 26-47; reprinted in Hoffmann and Fleron (1971), 451-470.
SIMON, Herbert A. (1957): *Models of Man: Social and Rational,* John Wiley, New York.
——— (1959): "Theories of decision making in economics," *Amer. Econ. Rev. 49,* 253-283.
——— (1968): *The Sciences of the Artificial,* MIT Press, Cambridge, Massachusetts.
SKILLING, Gordon (1960): "Soviet and Communist politics: a comparative approach," *J. of Pol. 22,* 300-313; reprinted in Fleron (1969a), 37-48.
——— (1966): "Interest groups and communist politics," *World Pol. 18,* 435-451; reprinted in Fleron (1969a), 281-297.
———, and GRIFFITHS, Franklyn (1971): *Interest Groups in Soviet Politics,* Princeton University Press, Princeton.
SKINNER, B. F. (1957): *Verbal Behavior,* Appleton-Century-Crofts, New York.
SLUSSER, Robert (1967): "America, China, and the hydra-headed opposition: the dynamics of Soviet foreign policy," in (P. H. Juviler and H. W. Morton, eds.) *Soviet Policy Making,* Praeger, New York. 183-269.
——— (1973): *The Berlin Crisis of 1961,* Johns Hopkins Press, Baltimore.
SMITH, Jean Edward (1963): *The Defense of Berlin,* Johns Hopkins Press, Baltimore.
SMOLANSKY, O. M. (1965): "Moscow and the Suez Crisis, 1956: a reappraisal," *Pol. Sci. Q. 80,* 581-605.
SNYDER, Glen (1961): *Deterrence and Defense: Toward a Theory of National Security,* Princeton University Press, Princeton, New Jersey.
SNYDER, Richard, BRUCK, H. W., and SAPIN, Burton (1962): *Foreign Policy Decision-Making: An Approach to the Study of International Politics,* Free Press, New York.
SONTAG, J. P. (1970): "International Communism and Soviet foreign policy," *Rev. of Pol. 32,* 78-90.
"Soviet foreign policy in the seventies" (1973): papers of a symposium held at Stanford University, December 1972, *Survey 19,* No. 2, 101-244.
SPEIER, Hans (1961): *Divided Berlin; the anatomy of Soviet political blackmail,* Praeger, New York.
SPIRO, Herbert J., and BARBER, Benjamin R. (1970): "Counter-ideological uses of 'totalitarianism'," *Pol. & Society 1,* 3-21; reprinted in Hoffmann and Fleron (1971), 326-345.
STEINBRUNER, John D. (1970): *Some Effects of Decision Processes on Policy Outcomes: A Series of Experiments Using Policy Games,* MIT Center for International Affairs, Cambridge, Massachusetts.
——— (1974): *The Cybernetic Theory of Decision: New Dimensions of Political Analysis,* Princeton University Press, Princeton, New Jersey.
STEINER, Peter O. (1970): "The public sector and the public interest," in (Haveman and Margolis, eds.) (1970), 21-58.
STEWART, Philip D. (1969): "Soviet interest groups and the policy process," *World Pol. 22,* 29-50.
STONE, Philip J., DUNPHY, Dexter C., SMITH, Marshall S., and OGILVIE, Daniel M. (1966): *The General Inquirer: A Computer Approach to Content Analysis,* MIT Press, Cambridge, Massachusetts.
STRAUCH, Ralph E. (1973): *A Critical Assessment of Quantitative Methodology as a Policy Analysis Tool,* R-1423-PR/ARPA, The Rand Corporation, Santa Monica, California.

STRONG, John W. (ed.) (1971): *The Soviet Union Under Brezhnev and Kosygin: The Transition Years,* Van Nostrand-Reinhold, New York.

SWETS, J. A., TANNER, W. P., and BIRDSALL, T. G. (1968): "Decision processes in perception," in (R. Haber., ed.) *Contemporary Theory and Research in Visual Perception,* Holt, Rinehart & Winston, New York.

TALBOTT, Strobe (ed.), *Khrushchev Remembers,* Little Brown & Co., Boston, 1970.

──────, *Khrushchev Remembers: The Last Testament,* Little Brown & Co., Boston, 1974.

TANTER, Raymond (1972): "The policy relevance of models in world politics," *J. Conf. Res. 16,* 555-583.

──────, and ULMAN, Richard H. (eds.) (1972): *Theory and Policy in International Relations,* Princeton University Press, Princeton, New Jersey.

TATU, Michel (1969): *Power in the Kremlin: from Khrushchev to Kosygin,* Viking Press, New York.

THOMAS, Hugh (1966): *The Suez Affair,* Weidenfeld & Nicholson, London.

THOMAS, John R. (1962): "Soviet behavior in the Quemoy crisis of 1958," *Orbis 6,* 38-64.

────── (1969): "Soviet policy toward Communist China and the 1958 Taiwan Straits crisis," Ph.D. dissertation, George Washington University, Washington, D.C.

THOMPSON, James D. (1967): *Organizations in Action,* McGraw-Hill, New York.

TIGRID, Pavel (1969, 1970): "Czechoslovakia: a post-mortem," *Survey 73 and 74/5,* 133-164 (Part I) and 112-142 (Part II).

────── (1971): *Why Dubcek Fell,* Macdonald, London.

TRISKA, Jan (1958): "A model for study of Soviet foreign policy," *Amer. Pol. Sci. Rev. 52,* 64-83.

────── (ed.) (1969): *Communist Party-States: Comparative and International Studies,* Bobbs-Merrill, Indianapolis.

──────, and FINLEY, David (1965): "Soviet-American relations: a multiple symmetry model," *J. of Conf. Res. 9,* 37-53; reprinted in Jacobson and Zimmerman (1969), 19-42.

────── (1968): *Soviet Foreign Policy,* MacMillan, New York.

TUCHMAN, Barbara (1962): *The Guns of August,* MacMillan, New York.

TUCKER, Robert C. (1963): *The Soviet Political Mind: Studies in Stalinism and Post-Stalin Change,* Praeger, New York.

────── (1967a): "On the comparative study of Communism," *World Pol. 19,* 242-257; reprinted in Fleron (1969a), 49-63.

────── (1967b): "United States-Soviet cooperation: incentives and obstacles," *Annals 372,* 2-13; reprinted in Hoffmann and Fleron (1971), 294-307.

────── (1973): *Stalin as Revolutionary, 1879-1929; A Study in History and Personality,* Norton, New York.

ULAM, Adam B. (1959): "Soviet ideology and Soviet foreign policy," *World Pol. 9,* 153-172; reprinted in Hoffmann and Fleron (1971), 136-153.

────── (1968): *Expansion and Coexistence: The History of Soviet Foreign Policy, 1917-67,* Praeger, New York.

────── (1971): *The Rivals: America and Russia Since World War II,* Viking Press, New York.

U.S. CONGRESS (1960): *National Policy Machinery in the Soviet Union,* report by the Subcommittee on National Policy Machinery, Committee on Government Operations, U.S. Senate, 86th Congress, 2nd Session, Washington, D.C.

────── (1963): *Staffing Procedures and Problems in the Soviet Union,* study submitted by the Subcommittee on National Security Staffing and Operations to the Committee on Government Operations, U.S. Senate, 88th Congress, 1st Session, Washington, D.C.

—— (1968): *Hearings on Military Posture,* Committee on Armed Services, House of Representatives, 90th Congress, 2nd session, Washington, D.C.

VON NEUMANN, J., and MORGENSTERN, O. (1954): *Theory of Games and Economic Behavior,* John Wiley, New York.

WALD, Abraham (1950): *Statistical Decision Functions,* John Wiley, New York.

WEINER, Norbert (1961): *Cybernetics,* rev. ed., MIT Press, Cambridge, Massachusetts.

WELCH, William (1970): *American Images of Soviet Foreign Policy,* Yale University Press, New Haven, Connecticut.

—— (1973): "On certain critiques of my *American Images of Soviet Foreign Policy*," *Newsl. on Compar. Studies of Communism 6,* No. 2, 32-40.

——, and TRISKA, Jan F. (1971): "Soviet foreign policy studies and foreign policy models," *World Pol. 23,* 704-733.

WELLFORD, Harrison (1973): *Sowing the Wind,* Bantam Books, New York.

WELSH, William A. (1969): "A game-theoretic conceptualization of the Hungarian Revolt: toward an inductive theory of games," in (Fleron, ed.) (1969a), 420-465.

WELTMAN, John J. (1973): "Is there a paradigm in the house?" *Orbis 16,* 1043-1056.

WESSON, Robert G. (1969): *Soviet Foreign Policy in Perspective,* Dorsey Press, Homewood, Illinois.

WHALEY, Barton (1973): *Codeword BARBAROSSA,* The MIT Press, Cambridge, Massachusetts.

WHITE, Ralph K. (1965): "Images in the context of international conflict: Soviet perceptions of the U.S. and the U.S.S.R.," in (H. C. Kelman, ed.) *International Behavior,* Holt, Rinehart & Winston, New York, 236-276.

WHITSON, William W. (1973): *The Chinese High Command: A History of Communist Military Politics,* Praeger, New York.

WILDAVSKY, Aaron (1962): *Dixon-Yates: A Study of Power Politics,* Yale University Press, New Haven, Connecticut.

WILLIAMSON, Samuel (1969): *The Politics of Grand Strategy: Britain and France Prepare for War, 1904-1914,* Harvard University Press, Cambridge, Massachusetts.

WINDSOR, Philip, and ROBERTS, Adam (1969): *Czechoslovakia 1958: Reform, Repression and Resistance,* Chatto & Windus, London.

WOHLSTETTER, Albert, and WOHLSTETTER, Roberta (1965): "Controlling the risks in Cuba," Adelphi Paper 17, Institute for Strategic Studies, London.

WOHLSTETTER, Roberta (1962): *Pearl Harbor: Warning and Decision,* Stanford University Press, Stanford, California.

—— (1965): "Cuba and Pearl Harbor," *For. Affairs 43,* 691-707.

WOLFE, Thomas W. (1970): *Soviet Power and Europe, 1945-1970,* Johns Hopkins Press, Baltimore.

—— (1973): "Soviet interests in SALT," in (William Kintner and Robert Pfaltzgraff, eds.) *SALT: Implications for Arms Control in the 1970's,* University of Pittsburgh Press, Pittsburgh.

YALEM, Ronald J. (1973): "Prolegomena on the post-behavioral revolution in international studies," *Orbis 16,* 1032-1042.

YOUNG, Oran R. (1969): *The Politics of Force: Bargaining During International Crises,* Princeton University Press, Princeton, New Jersey.

ZAGORIA, Donald S. (1962): *The Sino-Soviet Conflict 1956-1961,* Princeton University Press, Princeton, New Jersey.

ZARTMAN, I. William (ed.) (1970): *Czechoslovakia: Intervention and Impact,* New York University Press, New York.

ZIMMERMAN, William (1969): *Soviet Perspectives on International Relations, 1956-1967,* Princeton University Press, Princeton, New Jersey.

────── (1970): "Elite perspectives and the explanation of Soviet foreign policy," *J. of Int. Affairs 24*, 84-98; reprinted in Hoffmann and Fleron (1971), 18-30.

────── (1972a): "Hierarchical regional systems and the politics of system boundaries," *Int. Organization 26*, 18-36.

────── (1972b): "The transformation of the modern multistate system: the exhaustion of Communist alternatives," *J. of Conf. Res. 16*, 303-317.

────── (1973): "Soviet foreign policy—a new perspective," *Survey 19*, No. 2, 188-198.

ZINNES, Dina A. (1966): "A comparison of hostile behavior of decision-makers in simulate and historical data," *World Pol. 18*, 474-502.